All That I Am

All That I Am

Stinson E. Humphrey

Order this book online at www.trafford.com
or email orders@trafford.com

Most Trafford titles are also available at major online book retailers.

Printed in the United States of America.

ISBN: 978-1-4269-5547-1 (sc)
ISBN: 978-1-4269-5548-8 (hc)

Library of Congress Control Number: 2011900789

Trafford rev. 03/11/2011

 www.trafford.com

North America & international
toll-free: 1 888 232 4444 (USA & Canada)
phone: 250 383 6864 ♦ fax: 812 355 4082

Contents

Dedication

In grateful memory of my parents
who taught me to love

and

For Arvie
who is my love
forever and ever

Acknowledgments

First, I express appreciation to my sisters, Susan Perkins and Edna Rachel Miller, who wrote the afterword for this book, but who also became immersed in the project from the very beginning. In countless communications, they answered my questions, refreshed my memory and added immeasurably to the telling of our parents' story. They were always there to offer love, encouragement and support. With kindness and grace, they provided emotional support. We were blessed to grow up in a loving home and I am blessed to have two wonderful sisters whom I love and admire.

I extend my heartfelt appreciation to Dr. Kenneth Eakins, archaeologist, professor, physician and author of, among other books, *Becoming One,* who wrote the foreword for this book and who guided, advised and encouraged me at every step of the way. He understood the emotion involved in writing such a book and as such was able to provide a unique perspective. His unqualified support and genuine understanding of this project were invaluable, giving me purpose and direction throughout. He was an intimate friend of my parents and I am pleased he has been my friend and mentor for many years.

I am most grateful to Professor Osadolor Imasogie, past President of the Nigerian Baptist Theological Seminary and author of *Nigerian Traditional Religion* and *Guidelines for Christian Theology in Africa.* He offered encouragement and kindness as well as many valuable suggestions. His support and understanding of this project stemmed from an intimate knowledge and relationship with my parents of sixty years. I have known Professor Imasogie since childhood and am pleased he has been my friend for many years.

I am indebted to Dr. Joseph Ilori, Past President of the Nigerian Baptist Theological Seminary who was my contact in Nigeria and instrumental in providing me with many of the facts behind the story.

He conducted interviews with former students and is shepherding the publication of this book in Nigeria. He has been an integral part of the story itself, for well over a half century. I am most grateful for his additions, guidance, kindness and support throughout the process and am pleased to count him as my brother and lifelong friend.

A large debt of gratitude is due Roger Rule, historian and author of *The Rifleman's Rifle* and *Sarah* as well as four other books. His kindness, patience and energy gave me purpose and hope. I appreciate his wisdom, expertise and knowledge. His encouragement from the very beginning gave me the confidence at just the right time to push ahead with the project. I am grateful for his persistent encouragement to proceed toward completion of telling a story I long felt needed to be told.

I was fortunate to have Peggy Macedo, a retired schoolteacher, who was kind enough to read the entire manuscript twice during the time it was being prepared. Her expertise and unique writing skills were invaluable. Her many valuable suggestions and recommendations made my task much easier. Throughout, she offered encouragement and support when needed most. I am grateful for her advice, expertise, kindness, patience and good humor and am blessed by her friendship.

The task of accumulating images and insuring accuracy of my own memories was made easier by members of my extended family, including my aunts, Louise Oliver and Willa Gray Watkins, and my cousins, John David McGee, Marvin Humphrey, Marcia Morris, Carol Lehman, Norman Graham and Irving Graham.

My deepest gratitude is for my wife, Arvie. For over forty years, she has been my loving companion, friend, and confidante and has encouraged my every effort including her enthusiastic support in the writing of this book. She offered a unique perspective having known and loved my parents for the great majority of our lifetimes. She read the entire manuscript numerous times offering many valuable suggestions and insights as well as insuring the accuracy of my memory. Throughout, her contributions and encouragement came from love in an effort to insure I told the story with the sensitivity and love it deserves.

Foreword

by J. Kenneth Eakins

Some stories cry out to be told. <u>All That I Am</u>, an inspirational and skillful blend of text, letters and photographs presents that kind of story. Our world is blessed by the publication of this remarkable book by Stinson Humphrey.

<u>All That I Am</u> (every reader will be impressed by the total appropriateness of the title) is a true love story. First and foremost, it is a story of God's love and how Stinson's parents, Edward and Rachel Humphrey, participated eagerly with God in the ministry of sharing Divine love with the people of Nigeria and also with persons living in other parts of the world, including California. In addition, the book relates the intensely moving story of the very special conjugal love that forged Edward and Rachel into true oneness.

I first met the Humphreys in 1970 when my family and I moved to California in order for me to accept a position on the faculty of Golden Gate Baptist Theological Seminary in Mill Valley, where Edward had been teaching for four years. Also, my family and I soon joined Tiburon Baptist Church where the Humphreys were members. From the first, my wife, Marian, and I were drawn to Edward and Rachel. We felt a deep kinship of spirit as we observed them at the seminary and at church.

As a new faculty member at the seminary, I began quietly to "size up" my colleagues. Very soon I recognized that Professor Humphrey combined a very keen intellect and academic brilliance with a genuine modesty and a true humility that was very appealing. Readers of this book will discover—if they don't already know—that he had pursued his many years of higher education with a persistence and diligence that can only be admired. And Rachel, always his Darling, had encouraged him at every step of the arduous journey.

I gradually learned about their years on the mission field in Nigeria, and was filled with respect and gratitude for their devotion to that very important ministry and for their love of the people there. Quite clearly, this couple, new friends of mine, were choice servants of the Lord. You will be blessed as you read about their life in West Africa, and you will surely mourn with them as that phase of their ministry was forced to conclude.

Much that passes for love today is an impostor. However, it was clear to me from the beginning that the love I observed between Edward and Rachel was pure and authentic. Their love for one another was born of God's love. Divine love (<u>agape</u>) is unconditional, is active (not just words), and is unselfish. It is quick to make any needed sacrifices for the well-being of the one loved. Edward and Rachel were a living demonstration of this type of love, a love that results in true oneness of husband and wife.

In this area, my wife, Marian, and I felt a real closeness to the Humphreys. We, too, had a long marriage that was characterized by deep, mutual love and genuine oneness. And Edward and I both experienced the searing pain of seeing our loved one encounter serious illness and die much too soon (from our limited, human perspective). Marian died in August of 1990 following a five and one-half year long battle with breast cancer, and Rachel's death occurred in October of 1992. They went Home. Rachel's long struggle with multiple sclerosis is chronicled with tenderness and sensitivity in this book by her son, and we can all learn important lessons from her (and Edward's) example.

After the death of Rachel, Edward and I spent much time together reflecting on the nature of love and marriage. We often talked on the phone, wrote numerous letters to one another, and were able occasionally to meet for lunch. Those were important times for each of us. The man whom I came to know increasingly well and with ever-growing appreciation is the one presented so beautifully in <u>All That I Am</u>. Whether the readers already know the story of Edward (and Rachel) or are meeting them for the first time, they will be blessed.

A real treasure in this book is the Afterword, written by Stinson's two sisters, Susan Perkins and Edna Rachel Miller. Their comments about their parents are full of love and insights that definitely enhance the picture of Edward and Rachel and help make the book a "family report." How wonderful it is to read a true story where the relationship between children and parents is so suffused with authentic love! The message it contains provides a much-needed word for all people today.

Many books have appendices. These contain necessary and important information but are often dry, dull, and boring. The appendices found in All That I Am, however, sparkle with brilliance and are intensely moving. If you are among those reading this material for the first time, expect to shed some tears--but they will be tears of joy! If you have read some or most of these items before, you will still be stirred to the depth of your being. This book concludes in a crescendo of marvelous beauty! One cannot imagine a more suitable close to this magnificent story of faith, hope, and love—and the greatest of these is love (see I Corinthians 13:13).

Edward Humphrey loved Robert Browning's phrase, "One Word More," and quoted it often. It is fitting that Stinson uses this as the title of Chapter 15 and that he discusses the significance of these words for his father. In a very real sense, this volume by Edward's son presents readers with a most welcome "One Word More." Thank you, Stinson!

There are, however, other words—words of surpassing beauty. Edward and Rachel loved music. Now, as part of a Heavenly Choir, they are blending their voices with many, many others and singing words of praise to their Lord in songs that will be repeated throughout eternity. Readers of All That I Am will surely want to one day be part of that choir!

Introduction

When I was growing up, I knew the day would come when I would be required to leave home to continue my education on my own, well before I felt prepared to undertake a change of such magnitude. My parents were missionaries in Nigeria, West Africa. I was born there, reared in a sheltered, cloistral environment far different from contemporaries in the United States. For me, however, that resulted in an idyllic childhood and adolescence that continues to conger treasured memories. The nature of that environment produced a happy, confident young man ready to face the world, yet I dreaded leaving the security of a home where love was openly and freely expressed, where affection was demonstrated daily, and where a premium was placed on high moral standards and on the values of leading a faith-based life. At sixteen, my parents and sisters took me to the airport in Lagos (LAY-gus), the capital city of Nigeria at the time, and in what seemed like minutes, my life changed forever. The last hugs and expressions of love had come all too quickly as I found myself on a Pan Am jet, my face pressed against the window, staring for one last glimpse of the ones who had always been there for me and who meant the world to me, wondering if I could possibly stay just one more year. I tried unsuccessfully to hide the tears running down my face. It was to be two years before they would return to the states on a one-year furlough.

As we lifted off into the African sunset, I had no way of knowing of the events to take place so soon. Two months later, the phone rang in the boarding house where I was staying and someone said, "It's your father." I knew phone service did not exist where my parents lived. Was it a cruel joke? On the other end, it was my father, and as I tried to absorb what he was saying, my mind clouded. My body went numb. Soon the tears streamed again. At the time, he was unable to tell me with any detail the extent of my mother's illness, but I was very certain of one thing. They would not be back in the states unless the situation was very serious. That he left unsaid, for I knew the depth of my parents' life-long commitment to missions.

This book is the true story of my parents, ordinary and common people who shared an extraordinary and uncommon love. It is a story my sisters and I long encouraged my father to write for we have never been able to equal his expressive beauty and eloquence with words. Yet, for many years, I knew I would be the one to write this book, for my father was far too humble, too unpretentious to set pen to the telling of his own love story. It is a story that begs to be told, must be told and in the telling will be a great success if it helps but one couple struggling to live life more fully in the presence of a severe chronic illness of one spouse.

After they left Africa, my parents retained their shared divine calling to a ministry of faith and love, but it was to be in a far different place, and in far different ways from what they had once dreamed. Nevertheless, it was just as heartfelt and loving as their original dream. Naturally, the change in their lives affected the lives of all family members and, soon, the reunited family was living in a place about as different from West Africa as it could possibly be. That change in location allowed two missionary kids (MKs) to resume a relationship resulting in their marriage, creating a unique love story of their own. My wife, Arvie, also born to missionary parents who served in Africa, had a loving relationship with my parents who cherished her unwavering, sweet love and support throughout their lives. Arvie continues to love, care for, and support me in the disability I now face, and she is the one with whom I share three loving children (Rachel, Carol and John) and three wonderful grandchildren (Sadie, Tyler and Lilly).

Fortunately, my parents left many letters and writings of their own that I have used freely and liberally to better tell their story. Unfortunately, my mother lost her ability to write more than twenty-five years before her death, which may cause readers to feel as if an emphasis has been placed on my father's unique ability to express his thoughts in writing throughout the book. Nothing could be further from the truth. As in many families, she was the glue, the one always there, and the one who confided in me the stories about their love that he would never tell. What is clear in the written words she left is a deep love and devotion to her husband, to her family, and above all, to God, as well as their utmost trust and faith in Him and their shared commitment to a spiritual life. What was even more abundantly clear was the evidence of her faith and love through the many years during which she never complained when faced with unimaginable adversity and the unspoken communication from her eyes and heart long after she lost the ability to speak. That communication does not avail itself to copying onto paper or scanning into a computer. It remains in my heart very simply as my mother's love.

Many books tell the stories of spouses in which one develops a chronic illness that forever alters either the life of the other or the relationship itself. Many of these contain guidelines, concepts, strategies, and practical advice about coping with the stress that comes with caring for a loved one with a chronic illness. Most are books that attempt to share a story in order to make it easier for others with similar stories. Others are about emotional pain, loss of companionship, financial devastation, grief, and fear. This is a book not about coping with a chronic illness but about continuing to live in love and most importantly to live with and in the love of God. It is a story that will bring in some measure an understanding of both mortal and eternal love when faced with the severe illness of one spouse.

I have written this book to honor my parents and in so doing to offer grateful tribute to their memory and the ideals set forward by the example of their lives. My father often wrote of his love for my mother, his "Darling," but he also left us a written legacy of the ideals of his parents and their teaching and the example they set for others by the way they lived their lives. Moreover, he expressed the hope that his own grandchildren might know those same ideals and examples and pass them on to their own generation in some way. Therefore, at the beginning of each chapter I have included a quote concerning love from my father's writings that defines some of the content within the chapter but more importantly directly passes from generation to generation the very message of love he learned from his parents and yearned to pass on to succeeding generations. Some of these quotations are from letters he wrote. Most are taken from his book, *The Form of Godliness*.

The first portion of the book acquaints the reader with the early lives of Edward and Rachel Humphrey, their education and their dreams of a shared ministry through foreign missions. Their story then continues in a more general way with their lives as missionaries in Africa, followed by the onset of my mother's multiple sclerosis, which changed their career and led to a new, shared ministry. The story describes their experiences as they struggled to endure the ordeal of a severe, debilitating, chronic illness and the way they lived through it with trust and faith in God, and always with hope and love. Throughout, my hope is to express my undying gratitude for the example they set for me, living as *one* in the sight of God. They viewed their togetherness and their story of love as a symphony of love, one never to be finished. Their symphony lives on, not only in my mind and heart but also through all of eternity, a heavenly harmony of love.

The Libreville

*To love is to allow God to determine for us the object of our love
and let Him love that object through us.*

On a bright, warm summer afternoon on Thursday, June 17, 1948, Edward and Rachel Humphrey, newlyweds of little more than a year, stood on the dock of the harbor in New York City. Their hearts filled with excitement and anticipation as they gazed in awe at the Libreville, a Norwegian freighter on which they would begin the journey of their long-held dreams to serve as missionaries in a far-off land. Destination: Nigeria, West Africa! Quite a journey was in store for the young couple, whose lives had joined through love for one another and a deep desire to serve God through foreign missions. Along with their "loads"—clothing, food staples, books, general household goods, and enough supplies to last for three years—one other passenger, Miss Lavonna Lee of the Sudan Interior Mission, and the ship's crew, they quietly sailed out of the harbor as night began to fall. Their joy knew no bounds!

For several days, excitement had built as Edward and Rachel attempted to comprehend the sights, sounds, and wonders of a bustling New York City. Busily, they set about looking after the myriad of details required of them to embark. Departing their homeland for the first time required tending to and arranging for details that North Carolinian country farm folk were unaccustomed to—confirming international travel reservations, getting immunizations, and insuring that all their earthly belongings were aboard the ship. In an immediate, post-WWII world, the couple, both raised in poor families through the Great Depression, ventured with trepidation into the unknown. But theirs was a calling engendered in their youth, born of a deep faith and trust in God, a sense of service to others, and an abiding love for one another that, over the years, would be tested beyond measure.

Sleep came restlessly that first night at sea. Excitement, imagination, and questions raced wildly through their minds. What would Africa and Africans be like? How would the Africans accept them? Where would they live? How would they adjust to life as missionaries? Family, friends, home, and the familiarities of everyday life were slipping from a comfortable proximity as the Libreville sailed ever farther from shore. They would have almost four weeks to ponder the questions, anticipate the unknown, and absorb the excitement. Their attention quickly focused on daily living in close quarters among strangers, on the vastness of the open sea, and on the occasional school of flying fish as they learned to use a new camera, read, rested, and played checkers. Days of sunshine and calm seas gave way to howling winds and storms as the ocean rolled by beneath them. They marveled at the power of the surging waves as the ocean sprayed across the decks. Indeed, they thought, *It is a great God who can make and control the sea.*

As they headed toward Dakar, Senegal, the idle days at sea passed slowly. Anxious anticipation of life in the land of their dreams yielded to occasional thoughts of family and mothers left in tears. Yet a supreme sense of fulfillment embraced them as they began the realization of their dreams, for they would soon see the land they already loved. Appointment as missionaries to Nigeria, West Africa, by the Foreign Mission Board of the Southern Baptist Convention had come on April 6, 1948, and culminated years of education, praying, and planning. Edward wrote in his diary that they were "ready to venture upon the high road of (their) divine calling."

The evening of Tuesday, June 29, 1948, brought their first glimpse of Africa. Lights twinkled on the shoreline of Dakar as the ship's motors became quiet and they drifted silently and slowly toward port. The following day, Edward and Rachel set foot on the African continent, thrilled with excitement but desperately trying to absorb a vastly different culture. Back on board after a few hours spent on shore, they shared mixed emotions at what they had witnessed. The costumes of the natives were varied and unfamiliar. Poverty was everywhere. As the beggars, many of whom were small children, pressed close, they experienced the emptiness and hurt of an inability to respond. Perhaps the most vivid impression that first day ashore was the worshipping Muslims, falling to their knees, then prostrate with foreheads pressed against the hot pavement in murmuring, fervent prayer. The first impressions of Africans had been extensive and profound as they knelt in prayer that night, beseeching, "Oh, God, help us to love them and minister to them in the name of Christ."

A day later, back at sea, Rachel, who had been seasick most of the trip, seemed more than ever unable to keep food in her stomach. Her illness, which they attributed to the highly seasoned Norwegian food, ultimately proved to be her first pregnancy, but they were only beginning the third week of their journey and her persistent symptoms caused Edward to become more and more anxious to arrive. There were two more ports in Ghana, Takoradi and Accra, where their vessel docked for unloading and loading of new freight before they would reach Lagos, Nigeria. The now-familiar groups of "small boys," usually nude, begged for anything and everything—clothes, shoes, and money. A few days later, during the early morning hours of July 10, 1948, the Libreville drifted slowly and quietly into the port at Lagos.

In Rachel's words, "The voyage was one of excitement, of joy, of anticipation, and preparation. I believe the Lord continues to prepare us from one day to the next for what He has in store for us. Our hope was realized when we were appointed, our dream fulfilled, when we first saw the harbor at Lagos, Nigeria." After giving prayerful thanks to God, they prepared to disembark, ready to begin the mission work of their shared dreams and aspirations.

After clearing Nigerian customs, they were greeted by members of the Sudan Interior Mission who had come to meet their fellow passenger, Lavonna Lee. The Nigerian Baptist Mission was engaged in its annual mission meeting up-country. Therefore, they spent the weekend with the missionaries from the Sudan Interior Mission who met them. Undaunted, filled with faith and joy, they were ready to begin their three-year tour of duty in a foreign land that would become home amongst people they would quickly come to love.

Three years earlier, Rachel's older sister and her husband had arrived as missionaries in Nigeria. John and Doris McGee had recently returned to North Carolina for a one-year furlough but had left their U. S. Army jeep in Lagos for the Humphreys to use while they were away. After collecting their loads, Edward and Rachel found themselves driving toward what would be their first home in Nigeria, the small village of Iwo (EE-wo). Edward had little driving experience, having never owned an automobile, but Rachel had no experience. On unfamiliar, single-lane, unpaved roads, he drove the jeep very slowly on the left side of the road. Nigeria was a British colony with the British system of driving on the left. The trip to Iwo was a slow one by necessity, but they were happy, in love, and confident in the certainty of their calling.

The trip of about one hundred miles from Lagos to Iwo took two days with overnight stops at the homes of other missionaries. The new and diverse culture was immediately upon them as they journeyed inland, for the Oro festival had recently begun. The annual seven-day celebration of the worshippers of the pagan god Oro, believed to be the executor of criminals, was a stark reminder they were in the midst of a heathen culture. Oro worship was characterized by the whirling overhead of a thin, flat piece of wood or metal fastened to a cord. Whirled at high speeds, it made a loud whining noise. This was used as a means of keeping women and girls in subjection as the festival was a time during which females ventured from their huts only on the pain of death, according to Reverend Samuel Johnson, author of *The History of the Yorubas.*[1] The "aja Oro" (Oro's dog) howled all night their first night in Nigeria—an eerie reminder of why they had been called and why they had left family, friends, and the familiarity of rural North Carolina to go to Africa.

Once in Iwo, Edward and Rachel received temporary teaching assignments at the Baptist College of Iwo and spent two months in language study, familiarizing them with the Yoruba language. Stationed in Iwo for six months, they immersed themselves in teaching at the teacher training college for lower and higher elementary school teachers and at an industrial school, where students learned trades and modern farming techniques. They would soon be transferred to a new assignment but for now, they reveled in the happiness of realizing their long held dreams. Their service to Him was underway in Africa!

---

[1] Rev. Samuel Johnson, *The History of the Yorubas,* (London: Lowe & Brydone Ltd, 1969), 32.

Rachel on board the Libreville, 1948

Edward on board the Libreville, 1948

Early Life

*I am convinced that 'family' is the richest human treasure
of our existence.*

The year 1918 brought an end to World War I, followed closely by the gaiety of the "roaring twenties." In American history, it was generally a time of prosperity and optimism. The Model T, advent of the movie and the first transatlantic flight made the times a period of great social and technological advancement. Edward and Rachel were born during this period, but early life on the farm in rural North Carolina represented a far different lifestyle than the prosperity and optimism experienced by many within the country. Life on the farm represented workdays extending from sunrise until sunset with a break between to attend school. Life was hard but their family life and the values instilled by their parents gave them a different kind of prosperity and optimism— one they would never consider exchanging for a more materialistic lifestyle.

Although the Great Depression was yet to come, Edward Humphrey and Rachel Thompson were born into poor, struggling families. Life was hard and would remain so throughout their childhoods. However, in their minds, they were rich, for they were surrounded by love. Both were members of families who placed great value on their love for one another, education, family traditions and the wholesome values of a faith-based life. Both families placed a strong emphasis on living Christian lives with Christian values. Sundays were days of church going, Bible study and restful, enjoyable time with other members of the family. Church and Bible study were integral parts of family life. Despite their economic status, they found a goodness and tenderness in God's love and in the love of their families. Each of their earliest memories revolved around the importance of living a Christian life with Christian values. As such, each of their lives became a testimony of triumphant love and hope.

Early roots of the Humphrey family

The Humphrey family roots are in Robeson County, North Carolina. James Edward Humphrey was born March 2, 1918 to Stinson Earl Humphrey[2] and Caroline Patterson Graham Humphrey.[3] Edward's paternal grandmother, Eliza Frances (Fannie) Nicholson Humphrey,[4] a registered midwife, attended his mother at his birth. In so doing, her name is recorded in that capacity on his birth certificate. Fannie's husband, Neill Townsend Humphrey,[5] Edward's paternal grandfather and one of the "pillars" of the small local church, Tolarsville Baptist Church, died early in Edward's life. His strong religious character remained as one of Edward's earliest and most precious memories. Another was of his grandfather sitting on the porch of his home one Sunday afternoon reading his Bible. It made an indelible impression on Edward as a young boy who himself read the Old Testament twice and the New Testament five times during his teenage years. Another was of his grandfather walking down the road to visit his grandchildren in their home. Yet another vivid memory was of his grandfather lying on his deathbed. He was thought to have contracted "blood poisoning" after slipping on a porch freshly painted with lead-based paint. As one of his final requests, Neill asked that all his grandchildren gather around him. He simply wanted each of them to know how much he loved them and to say good-bye. It was a memory Edward carried with him all of his life, counting his own grandchildren as among the most precious of God's gifts, and relying upon the comfort of their presence when he neared his own death.

Family heritage

Stinson (Edward's father) was born in a log cabin into a farming family. Born in the wee hours of the night, his father, Neill, went outside to study the stars to determine if the birth had occurred before or after midnight for the family had no clock. Believing it must be past midnight, he assigned November 23 as Stinson's birthday.

Growing up on the family farm, Stinson was determined to pursue an education beyond high school. Because of limited financial resources,

---

2   Born: November 23, 1887; died: September 24, 1935
3   Born: March 4, 1894; died: December 16, 1951
4   Born: March 18, 1856; died: September 23, 1924
5   Born: 1861; died: July 29, 1924

he went door-to-door selling *The Harvard Classics*, which enabled him to attend college for two years at Buies Creek Academy (now Campbell University), and subsequently at State College in Raleigh, North Carolina (now North Carolina State University). He studied agriculture, in addition to his personal favorites, mathematics and Latin. After college and before he married, he worked for three years as a teacher in two rural schools, teaching primarily upper-level courses. As a teacher, he was a strong advocate of consolidating the numerous small rural schools of the county and busing the children to more centrally located schools. He believed this would provide better-equipped and better-staffed schools. At first, the idea seemed novel and too visionary to people in positions of more influence. However, this became the practice, which has prevailed to modern times.

Caroline (Edward's mother), the daughter of Gilbert Patterson Graham[6] and Mercy Parker Nye Graham[7], was born on a farm about three miles from the farm on which the Humphrey family lived. Gilbert died of throat cancer before Edward was born. Mercy, who Edward remembers most vividly of all his grandparents, lived until he was seven years of age. She requested that Edward's parents allow him to live with her for a few months when he was five and during this brief period, she made a lasting impression on him with her devout Christian faith.

Married in 1912 at the ages of twenty-four and eighteen, Stinson and Caroline lived in what had been his childhood home and on what was still the family homestead. For a few years, they ran the family farm successfully and were very happy in that role. What Stinson had learned about modern scientific farming principles during college he adapted to a successful and productive career on the farm for some seven or eight years. However, when the time came for his parents to divide the inheritance left to him and his sister, Lena, they suggested the two siblings be the ones to make the decision as to what each inherited. Stinson and Lena were very close all of their lives. He was known to affectionately address her with the endearing term, "Sister." Characteristically, neither of them wanted to choose, both going to great lengths to be fair. Their inheritance was the family home and a small number of stocks (equities) of approximately equal value. Aware that his sister also had a deep attachment to the old homestead, Stinson suggested that his sister be given the family home and he would acquire

---

6   Born: October 10, 1855; died: August 17, 1915
7   Born: February 13, 1867; died: September 14, 1925

the stock invested in nearby cotton mills in which he could work as a mechanic. That suggestion was the one ultimately decided upon and Stinson left the farm to work in the cotton mills where he maintained the machinery. He moved his young family to a small home in St. Pauls, North Carolina. However, it was not long before the stock was almost worthless when, in 1929, the financial crisis occurred that set in motion the Great Depression.

After selling his small home in St. Pauls for a pathetic price and with what remained of his savings, Stinson purchased a pair of mules and the necessary farming equipment to return to a life in farming, convinced that a rural environment was the most healthful and wholesome setting to rear a family. He therefore discontinued working as a mechanic but without the financial means to purchase a farm, resorted to farming as a sharecropper. Farming on land he did not own, he was forced to conform to the wishes and whims of uninformed landowners. Never again did he find the pleasure and enjoyment he once knew in what he described as "tilling the ground." During the depths of the Depression, Caroline somehow held home and family together, barely able to make ends meet. She accumulated empty flour and sugar sacks, and then cut, sewed and dyed them for appropriately colored fabric to make her children their clothing. In a labor of love, she laundered the clothes using an old-fashioned scrub board, then boiled them in an outdoor wash-pot and ironed them with "sad-irons" heated on the stove. She was determined to keep her children clean and presentable.

Stinson and Caroline's children remembered the tenacious spirit with which their parents met the challenge of the difficult years of the Depression. One of the more memorable incidents involved a cow they had on the farm that would produce as much as five gallons of milk per day. The milk produced by their cow provided one of the primary sources of nourishment for the family in the days leading up to the Depression and during some of the darker days of it. A scourge of tuberculosis attacked a large number of cattle in Robeson County, North Carolina. County officials required enforced testing of all cattle to rid the county of the deadly disease. Throughout his life, Edward vividly remembered the day their cow tested negative and how his parents wept for joy. As an adult, he was unable to speak of that day without the accompaniment of deep, teary-eyed emotion.

Life on the farm

Although an educated man, Stinson provided for his family through the meager, hard-earned profits of a sharecropper. Farming on land he did not own, a portion of his profits went to the landowners. It was a struggle to produce enough crops to provide adequately for his family's needs. All of the children worked on the farm both before and after school, often missing many days of school during harvest time. Stinson adhered to the principles of farming he learned in college in addition to those advocated in the publication *Progressive Farmer*. That periodical, with origins in Winston-Salem, North Carolina, was devoted to agricultural issues within the Tar Heel state. Founded in 1886, it offered essays with practical advice for farm families and included poetry, politics and humor that related to farming issues. Still published today, it was instrumental in advancing the latest techniques in agriculture and Stinson used it to his advantage.

Utilizing farming methods learned in college and reading the *Progressive Farmer,* he was able to double the average yield of some crops, especially corn and was among the first of local farmers to study and realize the value of soybeans as a crop of many uses. However, his landowners forced him to concentrate his efforts on the high profits of growing tobacco. Long before the health hazards of tobacco were known, Stinson became concerned by his own observations of the negative aspects of tobacco on general health but to no avail.

In their home on the farm, Stinson and Caroline kept many of the textbooks he had used during his education and in his earlier teaching career. Edward, who fondly and vividly remembered reading these books while growing up wrote, "Despite their modest means, our parents provided our childhood home with some of the world's greatest literature and encouraged us to avail ourselves of its benefits." These books included Caesar's *Gallic Wars* in Latin and Homer's *The Iliad*.

In his limited leisure time, Stinson read to Caroline and his children some of the great Scottish, English and American poetry. He had an unusual gift for rendering the rhythm and cadence of some of the more quotable poems—"Once upon a midnight dreary, while I pondered, weak and weary...Quoth the raven, 'Nevermore'." Some of those books of poetry remain as priceless heirlooms for his grandchildren, to be read and enjoyed for generations to come.

Early Christian faith

From Edward's perspective, even with the hardships of few earthly possessions, the Humphrey children "had the blessed privilege of sharing with our dear parents, in some small measure, the trials and the strains, the anxieties and the sweet joys of our family experience." Some of his earliest memories center on the Christian faith of his parents and grandparents. At the First Baptist Church of St. Pauls, North Carolina and subsequently at the small farming community church, Tolarsville Baptist Church, Christian faith was a central focus of the family. At the young age of eight, Edward along with his older brother, Earle, dedicated his life to God. Baptized into the Christian faith, they had openly identified themselves with "the family of God." Because Edward had learned in Sunday School of David Livingstone, the Scottish explorer and missionary to Africa, he became intrigued with the idea of work as a Christian missionary. Some years later, as a member of a mission and Bible study group for boys, he renewed his interest in Africa at age fourteen when he openly rededicated his life to Christian service "as God might lead". Caroline's sister, Edward's Aunt Annie Smith, whose "beautiful spirit was itself of far-reaching influence" in his life, led the study group. Many years later, he led his own study group in a discussion of the Bible and wrote:

> *The subject of the Bible is very dear to my heart. At an early age, I began a serious and consistent effort to become acquainted with its message. I read the Old Testament twice and the New Testament five times during my teenage years. Largely through Bible study, I was already keenly aware in my mid-teen years that God was calling me into His service. For some inexplicable reason, that call seemed almost from the beginning to be one to mission service in Africa.*

For many years, the only person in whom Edward confided his sense of calling to missionary service was his mother, Caroline. In Edward's own words, "I told no other person of this urge...I nourished this sense of divine calling in the depths of my soul. I dreamed and prayed for the time when I might venture 'upon the high road' of godly mission."

Unexpected family tragedy

Unexpected and violent tragedy struck the Humphrey family on September 24, 1935. In the prime of life, Stinson was killed in a car accident when a vehicle driven by an inebriated driver crashed into the car in which he was riding. Edward's younger brother John, the driver of the vehicle in which his father was a passenger, frantically attempted to avoid the oncoming vehicle in vain. Unjustifiably, he carried a sense of guilt about the accident the remainder of his life.

Edward became an adult that day. A few months short of his eighteenth birthday, he was now the primary breadwinner for the family. His older brother Earle had previously joined the Navy, a commitment he was required to keep. It therefore fell upon Edward to carry on the primary responsibilities of farming. First, however, were an unexpected funeral and the unsettling sight of his father's body lying in an open coffin, an ear stained by the drainage of dried blood. At the open graveside of his father, Edward drew on the foundation laid within his early life by his father and grandfather to build on his faith, rededicating his life to service through a ministry in foreign missions.

Financially devastated by the loss of its sole breadwinner, the family sought some measure of compensation within the legal system. The inebriated driver, who had caused the accident in which Stinson died, drove a company truck resulting in presumed liability by the company itself.　However, in the midst of the Great Depression, the family was unable to afford to hire an attorney. Ultimately, they settled the case for a pittance of $750.

The close-knit family joined in a common effort to continue farming without their father. Edward took over primary responsibility as a sharecropper. Although the younger children were still in school, each member of the family participated in a concerted effort to keep the farm running. Life on the farm was an arduous task when going to school but an even more formidable task was their efforts to keep the farm productive. Edward recalled assuming he would never graduate from high school because of the time commitment required to keep the farm producing. He attended school very few days, attempting to keep up by studying into the wee hours of the morning and going to school only to take required examinations. Fortunately, all the children had learned the lessons of life from parents grounded in hard work, responsibility, integrity and love of family.

On one occasion, Edward went into town to purchase a refrigerator on credit. The shopkeeper allowed him to have it on the promise that he would pay for it after the harvest. However, that year, the crops did not do well, whether for lack of fertilizer or weather. Nevertheless, he felt he must tell the man who had given him credit that he was not able to pay him for the refrigerator. The shopkeeper told Edward, "...bring me the money when you can." He never forgot the humiliation of that experience, avoiding any form of debt that he could and was forever sympathetic toward the poor, saying, "Nobody wants to be poor."

Although he attended school infrequently, Edward somehow managed to graduate from high school in 1936 at eighteen years of age. During this time, he kept the farm producing and for the following three years, he put on hold his desire to pursue higher education along with his ultimate goal of pursuing a career in Christian service as a missionary. He remained at home, assuming his father's responsibility for financial needs there until 1939. He kept a diary in which he made the paltry entries, "Plowed today," followed the next day by, "Plowed again" and then the next, "Did more plowing." Many years later, he wrote:

> *If only I had recorded what was all the while stirring within the depths of my soul! The thoughts and deep longings of my heart in those days were among the most profound and enduring of my entire life. In a real sense, I was already 'upon the high road' and did not know it. In later years, I was often thrown back upon the strength and assurance already being nurtured within me as I waited upon the Lord. I am now grateful for the restraints which were then imposed upon me.*

Parents remembered

In describing his father, Edward said, "he was the most transparently honest and upright man I ever knew. In mind, in speech and in manner of life, he seemed to be utterly without guile." Stinson was a man who believed that one could learn something from any and every other human being and himself, a man who seemed to rise above disdain for others in the throes of common everyday life. Among some of Edward's dearest memories were of his father's affectionate "good-byes" when he was leaving home, even if only for a day. His father had given those affectionate "good-byes" on the day he was so tragically killed in the automobile accident.

If ever there were a man who emulated that description, it was Edward himself although he would selflessly deny that he could ever live up to the standards set by his father. However, as husband, father and man, both Stinson and Edward were unfailingly kind, loving, supportive, and transparently honest. Both always put others and their needs before their own. In later years, Edward's siblings often spoke of Edward as the son most like their father.

Edward described his mother, Caroline, as "a kind and gentle soul" who "submerged her own life for the sake of her family" and was "in every respect the true complement" of her husband. Her children remembered her as a devoted companion to their father, a loving mother, one of the sweetest people in the world and an ideal companion for their father.

In Rachel, Edward found a wife and soul mate who seemed much like his own mother. As a wife, mother and woman, she, like Caroline, was kind, sweet, loving, nurturing, supportive and devoted to her husband. She was the ideal companion for him.

Stinson and Caroline Humphrey were proud of their family. All seven of their children remembered them with inexpressible gratitude, feeling they represented the near ideal of parenthood. They weathered the hard times of the Depression years with great courage and devotion to upholding their ideals and to raising their children with strong Christian moral values that represented their own.

Stinson Earl Humphrey, 1933

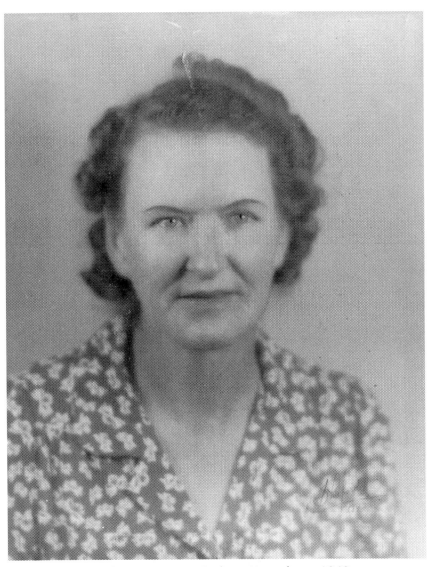

Caroline Patterson Graham Humphrey, 1943

Stinson Earl Humphrey, on the farm.

Edward, age 13, 1931

Edward, age 23, 1941

Edward (third from right) with his siblings – Gilbert, Louise, Thetis, John, Edward, Earle and Frances.

Early roots of the Thompson family

A remarkably similar family story was playing out not far away just outside Durham, North Carolina. On December 18, 1923, Sadie Rachel Thompson was born into the home of Early Graham Thompson[8] and Elsie Magnolia Holleman Thompson.[9] Recorded details of Rachel's early family life are limited.

Rachel's parents were born and reared in the rural community of Apex, North Carolina, a community in Wake County between Durham and Raleigh. She never knew her paternal grandparents, John Lewis Thompson[10] and Lettie Thompson,[11] or her maternal grandfather, Henry Holleman.[12] However, Rachel did know her maternal grandmother, Quinetta Segroves Holleman.[13] While Rachel was growing up, Quinetta lived with them as an integral part of the immediate family.

Rachel was the sixth of nine children born to Graham and Elsie Thompson. Before Rachel was born, her father, an insurance salesperson, gave up his job to move his young, growing family to the countryside, believing that environment to be a better, more wholesome one in which to raise his family. In a brief written statement about her life, Rachel noted, "My childhood was spent in the country, thus having all the opportunities of work, play and wholesome living that goes with country life."

Graham rented a large plantation-style home with a large amount of land—land put to good use with a quickly growing family. There was room for a vegetable garden, fruit trees, a henhouse to raise chickens and a pasture for two cows. Graham was an avid outdoorsman. Fishing and hunting, in part, helped keep his family fed but also led to his employment for several years as the county game warden. Later, as a more prosperous means of providing for his family, he managed a rural café with accompanying gas station, which he rented from the same property owner who owned the home that housed his family. The café and gas station were just across the road from the home. With long work hours, he was often home only to sleep and spent very little time with his children.

---

8   Born: November 19, 1888; died: March 6, 1936
9   Born: April 5, 1889; died: May 8, 1978
10   Born: July, 1864; died: unknown
11   Born: October, 1870: died: July 27, 1929
12   Born: March, 1855; died; August 23, 1922
13   Born: May, 1857; died: August 25, 1940

Elsie was the parent left to rear the children. She assigned each child individual chores and all the children rode the bus to attend the nearby local county public school. Memories of Elsie's children are that of a mother who worked hard, often struggling to meet the needs of her family. She worked from sunrise until late at night, not only to care for her family but also to help Graham in his fledgling café business. She used their large wood-burning stove at home to keep cornbread and other baked items available at the café. Working tirelessly, she sewed "making-over" clothes and canned fruits and vegetables grown in their large garden. Rachel remembered awakening one night to the sounds of someone crying. It was late and, as she crept ever so quietly to see who was crying, she saw her mother bent over her sewing machine, mending and making clothes not only for her own children but to bring in a little extra income. Seeing her mother crying from exhaustion and stress left an enduring impression on the young child. The same scene repeated night after night as her mother managed to provide the necessities of life.

The difficult economic times inhibited Graham and Elsie's ability to give their children all but the necessities of life. They encouraged their children to read in any spare time. A large collection of books discovered in the attic of their rented home together with the bookmobile that made its regular rounds, provided the children a great amount of reading material to fill their spare time. Reading, together with many afternoons spent playing with her siblings in a nearby river, left Rachel with memories of a happy childhood.

Early Christian faith

Rachel's family life revolved around the influences and values of a Christian home. Her parents were reared attending a Missionary Baptist Church and as such, she grew up with an interest in missions. She had close relationships with all eight of her siblings. There was never any doubt in their minds that their parents loved them deeply. A lack of transportation, common in the desperate economic times of the era, prevented the family from attending church on a regular basis. Yet some of Rachel's earliest memories are of her mother, Elsie, and maternal grandmother, Quinetta, reading the children Bible stories. Doris, an older sister who later also served in West Africa as a Baptist missionary, conducted Sunday School class for her siblings and the neighborhood children in their home. Beginning when Rachel was about ten years of age, her maternal uncle, Lassie Holleman, came every Sunday with his pickup truck to take the children to Grace Baptist Church in Durham. In 1934, at age eleven, she dedicated her life to God and was baptized on Christmas Day, later recalling, "That was the most wonderful Christmas I had ever had during childhood."

Unexpected family tragedy

Untimely tragedy befell the Thompson family in a similar manner as had occurred to the Humphrey family when on March 6, 1936 Graham suffered a massive stroke and soon died of complications of pneumonia. Rachel was twelve years old at the time but had vivid memories of realizing the hardships that lay ahead because of his death. Left with six hundred dollars after paying funeral expenses, Elsie could no longer afford to keep her family in the country. She moved her family into Durham and used the money to purchase land. Securing a loan, she built a small home. Her monthly payment of eight dollars and sixty-six cents was unaffordable without an income. Upon graduation from high school, each of the children assumed some of the financial responsibility for the family by seeking some form of employment.

In 1940, at age sixteen, Rachel too accepted this responsibility following her graduation from Bragtown High School. At the same time, she felt great personal conflict for she began to feel the "high calling" and with it a strong desire to begin preparation for special Christian work in foreign missions, but she was pulled by loyalty to her family and their financial needs. Although appointment as a foreign missionary required the pursuit of higher education, her family desperately needed the small amount of income she could generate. The financial hardship that existed before the death of her father became a reality of even greater proportion as she lacked any financial resources to begin college. She secured a special work grant that enabled her to begin work at age sixteen and for a year worked at several jobs, including Woolworths and in clerical positions for a dry cleaning company and an insurance company. For a year, she contributed essentially all of her income to family needs but never far from her mind was her commitment to Christian service and with it, the required education. Rachel attempted to save a small portion of her earnings to one day enroll in college. After working for a year, she had accumulated twenty dollars but during that year, she felt plagued by the nagging question, "Where does God want to use my life?" In a written statement on her early life and work several years later, she wrote:

> As I think back over the past, I think I knew the answer all the time but was not willing to accept it. In the mountains, I said 'Yes, Lord, the fields are white, even here.' But that was not the answer even though I would have liked for it to be. It was not until I said 'Lord, wherever you want me to go, I will go. Yes, even to the foreign fields.' At the age of eleven I gave my heart to Christ but at the age of twenty-two, I gave Him my life—and all was well.

The twenty dollars she saved along with a loan from a member of her church enabled her to begin her college education in 1941. She left for college with the blessings and emotional support of a grateful family who shared in her joy as she pursued her calling to serve as a missionary in a foreign land—perhaps India, she thought at the time.

Remarkable family similarities

The Humphreys and the Thompsons, two families with uniquely similar backgrounds, histories and circumstances were soon to become acquainted. In the presence of devastating economic times and premature deaths, both families had managed to nurture two individuals, relying on family values and a strong Christian faith. Both individuals had developed an abiding love of God and steadfast commitment to a calling to foreign missions. Nourished in faith by their families, Edward and Rachel each began college with the goal of Christian mission service, willing to follow God's plan to lead them to serve.

The importance of family heritage and family values were never far from Edward and Rachel's minds and hearts. Their love for family was a constant within their lives. In the eighth decade of life, Edward, reflecting on the word "family," wrote:

> I am convinced that 'family' is the richest human treasure of our existence. Normally, and ideally, family is the God-given context of human life from the moment of birth to the moment of death. Birth and death are the frontier-posts of our mortality. At birth, the helpless infant is taken up and loved and nurtured

and sheltered within the family unit. And at death, it is again the family unit that draws nearest in love and concern. When the subject 'family' is qualified by the very special adjective, 'Christian,' it is immeasurably enriched. The qualifier 'Christian' designates both the foundation and the divine purpose for this unit in society. It expresses the astounding idea that we are human helpers of God in the realization of His creative purpose in the world.

Early Graham Thompson, Rachel's father

Elsie Magnolia Holleman Thompson

Rachel's childhood home outside Durham, NC

Rachel age 4, 1928

Rachel age 13, just after
her father died, 1936

Rachel, age 16, 1940

Elsie, Rachel's mother, with all of her children - (Top L to bottom R)
Graham, John, Billy, Bobby, Lela Mae, Willa Gray, Elsie,
Rachel, Ruth, Doris

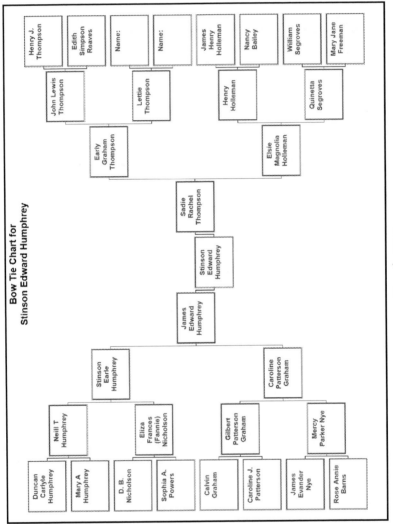

Bow Tie Chart for
Stinson Edward Humphrey

Henry J. Thompson
Edith Simpson Reaves
John Lewis Thompson
Name:
Name:
Lettie Thompson
Early Graham Thompson
James Henry Holleman
Nancy Bailey
Henry Holleman
William Segroves
Mary Jane Freeman
Quinetta Segroves
Elsie Magnolia Holleman

Sadie Rachel Thompson

Stinson Edward Humphrey

James Edward Humphrey

Stinson Earle Humphrey

Neill T Humphrey
Eliza Frances (Fannie) Nicholson

Duncan Carlyle Humphrey
Mary A Humphrey
D. B. Nicholson
Sophia A. Powers

Caroline Patterson Graham

Gilbert Patterson Graham
Mercy Parker Nye

Calvin Graham
Caroline J. Patterson
James Evander Nye
Rose Annie Barns

Family tree

Love and Marriage

Above all else, marriage (on both sides!) is a giving of all that one is to the other—literally, a submerging of self for the sake of the other.

Preparation for lives dedicated to God and foreign missions required Edward and Rachel to pursue higher education. They each went about this endeavor torn between loyalty to their families enduring difficult economic circumstances and their calling to foreign missions. In spite of their own personal emotional conflict, each went off to college with the love and blessings of their respective families.

On a wing and a prayer

After completing high school, Edward spent three years tenant farming to provide for his family's needs in his father's place. As younger siblings took over his responsibilities on the farm in the fall of that year, he enrolled in Wake Forest College to begin his undergraduate education. However, upon completion of his first year of college in the spring of 1940, family obligations forced him to interrupt his college career and once again resume financial support of his family, primarily that of his mother, Caroline, and his youngest siblings. Returning home, he found that his mother's health had deteriorated. His siblings were in pursuit of their careers and he therefore determined that a rural setting and farming were no longer suitable options. With the country engaged in World War II, Edward had first sought to join the war effort, feeling it his duty, but was turned down by the military upon discovery of a heart murmur. After moving his mother to Fayetteville, North Carolina, he worked briefly on a construction project at nearby Fort Bragg. However, in the midst of a wartime economy, he decided the best opportunities were further north where he could seek employment that would enable him to support his mother while saving what money he could to eventually continue his college education. Moving to Baltimore, Maryland, he worked at the Glenn Martin Aircraft Company for the next three years. Dutifully, he sent his mother eighty dollars a month, more than enough to cover her monthly rent. Of the time spent in Baltimore, he later wrote that "(he was) thrown back upon strength and assurance...being nurtured within...as (he) waited upon the Lord." Unknowingly, that strength and assurance were the pillars within his personal foundation upon which he relied many times in the years yet to come. Referring to the years spent in Baltimore many years later, he wrote, "I am now grateful for the restraints which were then imposed upon me. Our times are in God's hands, and He alone knows best when and where and how, one may render the greatest service to His glory." Certain his life was in God's hands, he felt he was "upon the high road."

Edward worked nearly three years in Baltimore before deciding he could return to Wake Forest College, which he did in January 1944, eager to resume his studies. He had managed to save four hundred and fifty dollars, which he carried with him in his pocket. The money he saved was in addition to eighty dollars a month he had faithfully sent home to his mother. In his heart, he carried "a determination to meet my long-held dream of obtaining my educational objectives in as expeditious a manner as humanly possible." He was approaching twenty-six years of age, keenly aware of the pressure of time. Ahead of him was the equivalent of three years of college education plus three years of postgraduate seminary education before the Foreign Mission Board of the Southern Baptist Convention would consider him for appointment to the foreign mission field. That appointment to the mission field carried a deadline—he must be no more than thirty-two years of age to receive appointment overseas.

Junior college

In the fall of 1941, Rachel left home to enroll at Wingate Junior College. The twenty dollars she had saved working at Woolworths was sorely insufficient and required that she seek student employment as well as a loan from a member of her church. She felt she "owed a debt of gratitude and love to (her) brothers and sisters who were willing for (her) to go to college, and (also) to my pastor who encouraged me throughout the days of my preparation." Preparation included volunteering for two summers as an educational director at her home church, Grace Baptist

Church, in Durham. During those summers, she was "sure that experience was of more help to (her) than (she) was to anyone in the church."

Rachel graduated from Wingate Junior College on May 29, 1943 with an Associate in Arts degree. Anxious to get to the mission field, she applied directly to the women's division of Southern Baptist Theological Seminary in Louisville, Kentucky. Had she followed through with that plan, she would have never met Edward but someone wisely advised her to complete her college education first. God's plan for her life was at work without her full understanding of its implications. In the fall of 1943, she transferred to Wake Forest College continuing to struggle in her mind with the lingering question, "Where does God want to use my life?" She was clear at that point in her life, that mission service was her future and was content to rely on God to lead her to the right area of service. She spent the summer of 1944 engaged in home mission work in the mountains of Kentucky working in coal mining communities and repeated that work in the summer of 1945, yet questions lingered in her mind. She knew she had "given (her) heart to Christ" at age eleven but felt she had not yet "given (her) life to Him." She would eventually do so at age twenty-two after working another summer for the Home Mission Board in the mountains of Kentucky. By this time, she had become acquainted with and was falling deeply in love with Edward.

Getting acquainted

On the opening day of spring semester, January 1944, three students arrived early for their first class. Edward, who was continuing with his college education after returning from Baltimore, was with Mary Gay, a friend with whom he became acquainted while at Wake Forest three years earlier. Speaking together casually, he found the other young woman present particularly attractive and engaging. After waiting patiently but far longer than he thought necessary, his friend Mary finally turned to him and said, "Edward, I would like you to meet one of my friends, Rachel Thompson." In the brief conversation that ensued, he learned his new acquaintance was also a mission volunteer! Until then, he had never met anyone, male or female, who was unequivocally committed to missions. Not surprisingly and quite naturally, a new friendship was born that day that rapidly evolved into a courtship. Love was in the air!

When they met, Rachel was in the middle of her junior year of college and Edward was beginning his sophomore year. The factor of time took on a new and additional meaning for him—he was playing catch-up in an attempt to graduate near the time she graduated. Resolved to reduce the time factor as much as he could, he took an unusually heavy academic load each semester and attended summer school each summer for three consecutive summers

Financing college education

College education was a financial hardship for both Edward and Rachel, but particularly for him. She financed her education by working in the college cafeteria, saving money earned during the summers and she received a loan from a member of her church in Durham. The money saved during the summers was by working first as a salaried educational director in her hometown church, and, subsequently, in the mountains of Kentucky, engaged in home mission work.

Edward, however, had no such benefactor, no time to seek student employment with the heavy academic load he undertook and therefore no ability to save money. Rachel tearfully recounted many years later the extreme financial hardship he endured by recalling he shared one room with a classmate, an attic room without heat. By necessity, showers were taken at the college gymnasium. Together, the two young men would break the ice on their pot of cooked beans to share their meals each day. At one point, they were out of money, unable to buy their usual fifty-pound sack of beans. Edward feared a premature end to his dreams of a college education and with it, abandonment of his calling to missions. Dejected, he walked to his campus mailbox hoping for a letter from home to pick up his spirits. To his amazement, he received a letter of encouragement from a member of his hometown church and with it a check for seven dollars. Exuberant, he carried a new sack of beans back to his room. Certain of his conviction that God had called him to foreign missions yet not always certain of his next meal he knelt in prayer. Somehow, he resolved to find a way to complete his education and his commitment to God.

Love blooms in the spring

Regardless of their financial difficulties, Edward and Rachel were fast becoming more than good friends with a common calling. They regularly studied together, took walks and enjoyed each other's presence when circumstances and time permitted. Realizing he was falling deeply in love with her, on one occasion he recounted, "I was already in our usual wing of the college library studying (when) I looked out the window onto a campus walkway and saw her coming. I remember the distinctly wistful thought: 'Would that she was even now walking into my life!' I think that it was generally understood around campus that she was my girl."

Rachel graduated from Wake Forest College with a bachelor's degree in May 1945. Edward continued in summer school but needed to spend an additional summer at Wake Forest to obtain his degree. In the fall of 1945, they moved to Louisville, Kentucky where both enrolled in the Southern Baptist Theological Seminary. Edward subsequently returned to Wake Forest the following summer to complete his bachelor's degree.

Rachel at Wingate, April 1943

Edward at Wake Forest, 1944

Rachel in her room at House Beautiful, 1945

Edward and Rachel at her mother's home, April 1945

Tuesday Morning
May 14, 1946

My pretty Darling,

You can count the days on the fingers of one hand now, and have one left over! — until I will be seeing the one I love so dearly. And don't forget, I am counting the days. Talk about a happy boy! "That's me." I have so much to be greatful for. God has called me into a wonderful work, and has given me the sweetest girl I know for a companion in it. You are in all of my dreams and anticipations, darling. Nothing in all the world is as precious to me as these things I am talking about now. I hope that we will continue in His will to the extent that He will be glorified in us every day of our lives. When our lives are brought together I hope that we will be daily finding new ways and areas of our lives that we can consecrate to Him.

I am going up with Earle, Ethel, John, Louise and Mama to see Frances today.

Letter from Edward to Rachel, May 14, 1946

37

2

We keep on the go so much that I don't get anything much done toward studying my sermons. And I don't get to see much of them unless I go with them where they go. I have lined up a tentative outline of sermons for the week, however. I am so anxious for it to be a success, and that some will be brought to the Saviour if it can be so.

Darling, I still plan to go over to Durham on Friday morning from W. F. to see you. I am already so excited about it that I can hardly wait to get started. I never wanted to see you so badly before as I do, and it keeps getting worse.

Mama was very proud of the picture you sent for her. She told me to give you her word of thanks, and to tell you that she treasured it greatly.

I am looking forward to seeing all of the good brethren and sisters at Wake Forest this week. We have some very dear friends

Letter from Edward to Rachel, May 14, 1946, page 2

there, don't we Darling? I love Wake Forest now much more than I did while I was there. It has done so much for me that I can never forget.

Precious, they are about ready to go, so I had better draw to a close now, I suppose. I want to say again that I love you with all that I am or ever hope to be, and I am every bit yours.

Give my love to all of the Thompsons.

All my love and life,

Edward

Letter from Edward to Rachel, May 14, 1946, page 3

Pastoral milestone

Before going to the seminary in Louisville in the fall of 1945, Edward acted publicly on his call to the ministry. Returning home, he was ordained in the presence of a proud family and many of those who had nurtured his calling to Christian ministry. He recorded on the inside cover of his Bible his ordination to the work of "The Gospel Ministry." It took place at the First Baptist Church of Lumberton, North Carolina on August 26, 1945. At the age of twenty-seven, James Edward Humphrey had become an ordained minister of God.

Symphony of love

During the mid-twentieth century, a theological education for women at the seminary consisted of studies leading to a master's degree in Religious Education. Rachel enrolled in the Women's Missionary Union (WMU) Training School division of Southern Baptist Theological Seminary. Edward worked toward his divinity degree. Their courtship begun while at Wake Forest, resulted in a relationship that continued to blossom at the seminary in Louisville. They took classes together whenever possible. As time permitted, their afternoon strolls in nearby Cherokee Park and evenings spent by the fire in the parlor of the WMU Training School dormitory, identified as the "House Beautiful" by male seminarians, led to an ever-deepening relationship. In Rachel's words, "We realized God was drawing our lives closer and closer together for a common purpose—for the accomplishment of a work in Africa." They fell deeply and forever, in love; a love strengthened and bound by their faith in God and His calling to foreign missions. In soft harmonious and melodic chords, a symphony of love was underway and soon led to Edward's proposal of marriage. Recounting his proposal, Edward wrote,

> One evening...I ventured over to 'House Beautiful' where Rachel was rooming. For some reason, I felt an even greater desire than usual...to be near her. She informed me right away that she had a few necessary chores to attend to that evening... but we went for what was to have been a short stroll in the pleasant night air. A short way from the living quarters, we turned about to retrace our steps to the dormitory. Then and there, for the first time in our acquaintance, I kissed her. She

immediately forgot that there were other matters demanding her attention, and we went for a leisurely, unhurried stroll.

On one of our many strolls in Cherokee Park one gorgeous fall afternoon, we were drinking in the rare beauty of God's handiwork in nature. The stately poplars and other trees along our path were aflame with yellow, orange and golden hues. Over-arching branches of those trees on either side appeared to form a magnificent vaulted passageway into some inviting, uncharted future. A small quietly gurgling stream meandered joyfully alongside as though to escort us into the forever and ever. That sylvan paradise seemed to match the enchanting whispers of our own hearts. And then we paused at one of the loveliest spots this side of Eden. I held her tenderly in my arms, looked deep into her lovely, limpid eyes, and asked: "Darling, will you marry me"? Her precious answer is writ large in the more than forty-five blissful years that God gave us in dear conjugal union."

Capriccio

Edward proposed during their first year at the seminary in October 1945. Although deeply in love, both were committed to completing their seminary education. Their education required a postponement of marriage but both felt a deep satisfaction in the assurance of their commitment to each other. Their individual dreams and longings for a life committed to missions now became a joint endeavor bound through faith and daily prayer together. It would be more than a year and a half before they would meet at the altar of marriage.

Secretly, Edward laid plans to purchase a symbol of their love and commitment to one another in the form of a diamond solitaire ring. Rachel was unaware when he visited a downtown jewelry store in Louisville to select the perfect ring to symbolize that love and commitment. She remained unaware as he began an oft-repeated game while holding her hand. Ostensibly as a mindless preoccupation, he would remove a friendship ring she wore on the second finger of her left hand. In the course of quiet conversation, he slipped the ring on his little finger, repeatedly playing with it but all the while measuring and memorizing exactly where on his finger the friendship ring fit. After a short while of playing his game, he was ready to return to the jewelry store where he made the first two-dollar payment on the diamond ring he had earlier selected. After some months, the payments were completed and the ring was now his to take to the love of his life, his darling. With the most precious purchase of his entire life tucked safely in his pocket, his excitement barely contained, he again sat with her that evening in the parlor of "House Beautiful". Holding her hand, he began the game to which she was now accustomed only this time exchanged her friendship ring with the diamond ring and slipped it on her finger. Agonizing moments passed, but then she noticed and in Edward's words, "went into orbit!" Though small and unpretentious, that ring, to them, was the most beautiful symbol of love in the entire world. In class together the next morning, the attention of neither was focused on the professor. They were eager for the world to know!

During their engagement of almost a year and a half, numerous love letters passed between the young lovers but none as prophetic as the one Edward wrote to Rachel on Christmas Eve, 1946. It would portend the future like no other while setting the tone for the manner in which they would forever view their marriage and commitment to one another.

Rachel, My Love,

Christmas-eve
1946

It is now 10:45 o'clock P.M. on the last Christmas eve night that I ever hope to spend away from you, my darling. I am listening to Christmas music on the radio and thinking about the one whose presence with me now would be more precious than gold, the one who has taught me the meaning of love. Rachel, your love has proved to be the purest and sweetest thing of all my life. It will be my joy to prove as nearly as I can through all the years what tongue and pen must ever be helpless to speak; Ah yes, Precious, and on after tongue and pen are still, my love for you will be but sweeter and more pure. I hope that one day we shall look back across the years through which we shall have come together and see that though there has been a commingling of the sad with the sweet, of the sorrowful with the joyful, we have endured as one soul, receiving all our strength from an all-wise and loving Father. And may we see in our wake a touch of beauty where there were ashes, and garments of praise where there was the spirit of heaviness. Rachel, I think that we shall then each look into the dimmed eyes of the other and read meanings too deep for tears, and then together lift our tired but happy faces even unto the face of God to catch the full splendor of Eternal grace. Could any prospect be more sweet to mortals on this Christmas-eve? Let us seek in this season a new and deeper Consecration to our great Calling.

Letter from Edward to Rachel, Christmas Eve, 1946

43

Pastoral ministry

Upon completion of his degree at Wake Forest in the summer of 1946, Tates Creek Baptist Church, the fourth oldest church in Kentucky, called Edward as pastor. The church, in Richmond, Kentucky (Madison County) would later become a Kentucky historic landmark. Founded in 1783, distant relatives of Daniel Boone had at one time been members. This calling provided a meaningful way for him to acquire some experience that would be later required by the Foreign Mission Board of applicants seeking appointment to the foreign mission field. He served as pastor for almost two years, resigning only weeks before departing for Nigeria. For over fifty years, Tates Creek Baptist Church was an important source of support and always remained in contact with the Humphreys. On each furlough from Nigeria, a special visit to the church was always on the calendar.

Rachel could not attend Tates Creek church because of her own obligations until Easter Sunday of 1947. For quite some time, the congregation had been eager to "lay eyes" on the pastor's fiancé. When the big day finally arrived, Edward carefully prepared for the occasion, presenting Rachel with a corsage accompanied by a note written the evening before.

On that particular Easter morning, Edward quickly noted that his sermon was not the main attraction. Vividly recalling the scene decades later, he wrote, "I had adorned her lovely person with a corsage of three yellow rose-buds, newly opening. To me, she was the very essence of charm and beauty and loveliness. And soon it was obvious to me that I had the enthusiastic approbation of my little flock, all around".

A few days later, Rachel received her Master's degree in Religious Education from the WMU Training School affiliate of Southern Baptist Theological Seminary. Returning home to Durham immediately thereafter, she prepared for their wedding. Edward soon followed to his mother's home in Fayetteville. Deeply in love, they exchanged numerous love letters on a daily basis during their short time of separation of which only a few of hers to him have survived over the years. On May 23, 1947, Edward and Rachel were united as *one* in Holy Matrimony.

Easter Eve

My Darling,

I passed far deep into the garden of love today, And paused at each turn of the way to re-live the moments which hallow those sacred spots to me. As I wandered I plucked a blossom here and there with which to adorn the Queen of My Heart.

Your,
Edward

Note from Edward to Rachel on Easter Eve, 1947

Edward and Rachel, April 1947

Monday Night
May 5, 1947

My Own Darling,

It seems such a long time since I had that awful sinking feeling when the hour did come when we were separated or for a time. Darling, when I think of how much longer it's going to be my heart is made more heavy. I love you so tonight- I long to be with you.

Today has been a busy one. Mother & I washed and I ironed, got ready for circle meeting. I enjoyed speaking to them but I sorta rambled. They gave me a little shower- 2 towels, lace, a slip, a sheet, pair of pants - there were just seven at the meeting.

Mrs. Pulley is planning a shower for me on next Monday night and Lula Mae & Phyllis is planning one for me Friday week night- People are sure nice to me and

Rachel to Edward, May 5, 1947 – two weeks before wedding

I wish they wouldn't do so much.

Darling, I didn't need the extra money, but I forgot to enclose it in my last letter. Thank you so much for it, I appreciate your thoughtfulness and kindness in loaning it to me.

I'm going to town in the morning and I'm hoping to find a suit. Most of them are on sale now greatly reduced. I think I'm going to try buying a hat, too, Lela Mae couldn't borrow a veil so I'm going to have to buy one, therefore I guess I'll have a short one. I probable will not know the difference.

Precious, I hope you have had a good day and you've accomplished a lot. Have you loved me lots today? I know you have, it was as swell to know that you do all the time. I know I love my darling with all my heart and if I could be with you for just a little while I would be content and happy. My heart is heavy for you.

God bless you, Darling. May God give you a good nights rest. I'm so tired. but as desperately in love. Your very own Darling

Rachel to Edward, May 5, 1947, page 2

Tuesday Night
May 6, 1947

Darling, My Darling,

Your first letter came this morning and I was so very glad to get it. You expressed so beautifully just how I've been feeling — "there is an aching void that all the world cannot fill" when you are away from me. Darling, I miss you so — My soul, too, reaches out for you tonight — but is not satisfied — I am thankful of one thing Darling — that we will not be separated all the summer. I don't know what I would do if we were for these days cause me to carry a heavy heart.

Rachel to Edward, May 6, 1947

"Precious, I love you tonight, with all my heart and soul I love you. My heart aches for you. Darling, take care of yourself and get all your socks darned before I come to live with you -

I wish I could tell you something of my love for you but I can't even begin - Just remember that I'm praying for you and thinking of you all the day -

My love, my all forever
Rachel

Rachel to Edward, May 6, 1947, page 2

Wednesday Night
May 7, 1947

My Darling Edward,

If it has been as pretty there today as it has here, you've been out working all day. I hope you are not too tired tonight. I am not quite as tired tonight as I was last night. We cut out a dress this morning after we caught up a few other loose ends. This afternoon I went to my second W. M. S. circle meeting of the week. I talked to them on Japan. I had a lot of material I could have used if it were not there. I got along fine, however.

It was nice of your church to let you off like this

Rachel to Edward, May 7, 1947

53

Sunday. Let me know when you plan to get here. I would definitely advise you to come the way I did. It is a much better way to come if you come to D.

I didn't get around to calling the health department today, But I will tomorrow. I want you to come by here like everything the first of the week but if it isn't necessary I ~~your mother~~ would like for you to come on home. How I want to see you!! I want you to come just as soon as you possibly can. It doesn't seem right not to see you and be with you. I look forward to your letters and enjoy them very much but they can never take the place of your presence. Last Wednesday night we were sitting in

Rachel to Edward, May 7, 1947, page 2

the moon light — so peaceful and
quiet and I was so content for
I was in the arms of my
most beloved. I love you
tonight, precious, with all
my heart!! And I miss you
so very badly. The hope of
being with you for always
in about two weeks keeps
me going - Always, Darling -
Always I'll have with you -
~~I love and cherish~~ -
Then, Darling you will learn
bit by bit of my love for
you. All along the way, our
love will continue to grow -
How can I tell you of my
heavy heart tonight?! It is
heavy for lack of expression
of what it feels to deeply -
I love my Darling - Be a sweet
boy - My thoughts, prayers and love
are with you day + night - all that I have'
now'

Rachel to Edward, May 7, 1947, page 3

Becoming *One*

The wedding was simple yet all they desired for to them it was the essence of beauty, representing their union as *one* before God and the entire world. Their respective families gathered in Durham joined by friends from both college and seminary. The wedding took place at Grace Baptist Church in Durham. In the absence of her deceased father, Rachel's eldest brother, Graham, accompanied her down the aisle to the marriage altar. Various siblings and friends from college and seminary served as bridesmaids and groomsmen. Also present was a soloist, an organist and a flower girl—Rachel's niece who many years later shared with her the diagnosis of multiple sclerosis.

The exchange of rings became the most significant aspect of the wedding ceremony and came to define their love and marriage in ways they could not understand or imagine at the time. In her ring, Edward had the inscription "My Darling" engraved, a term he forever used when addressing her. Rachel, however, set the tone for their marriage when she had engraved the inscription "All That I Am," words of an almost unimaginable depth of meaning, devotion and commitment. Recounting the ceremony many years later, he wrote,

> To me, the loveliest vision of all time was that of "my darling" approaching me at the marriage altar. And the most precious verbal exchange of our mortality was the utterance of those sacred vows with which we sealed our union. My joy (no, our_ joy!) knew no bounds! She was mine; and I was hers! And so it would be forever and ever. In the exchange of rings, the engraved inscriptions spoke again for all time the deepest and holiest sentiments of our hearts. In the ring I placed upon her finger were the simple words "My Darling." That she was, and ever shall be—the "Darling" of my heart. But, she said it best. In the ring which she placed upon my finger are inscribed the simple words: "All That I Am." Those precious words burned their way, long ago, into the deepest recesses of my soul. I thrill all over again upon every remembrance of them. For more than forty-five years, she demonstrated that it was all—and all that she was.

The ceremony concluded, they proceeded down the aisle of the church and out the front door to circle around the outside of the building and return to the front of the church for photographs. Decades later, Edward often told the story of how they were met by a barrage of water, fired from the water pistols of some "rascally neighborhood boys." Their faces dripping wet, he grabbed his handkerchief, quickly wiping his bride's pretty face. Photographs completed, Rev. and Mrs. Edward Humphrey returned to the home of the bride's mother, Elsie, for a small reception.

After saying their good-byes to family and friends, the newlyweds were off to a nearby hotel to spend their wedding night. Ever mindful of the constant and profound presence of God in their lives, they began their lives as *one* in the eyes of God by reading together the eighth chapter of Romans, scripture they had carefully selected beforehand. They had adopted that chapter to serve as a kind of biblical anchor for their marriage. Through the years, it continued to be a primary focus in their devotion "to (their) Lord." On each subsequent wedding anniversary, they read that chapter, choosing, in particular, the verses of Romans 8: 35-39[14] as their own.

> *Who shall separate us from the love of Christ?*
> *Shall tribulation, or distress, or persecution, or famine, or nakedness, or peril, or sword?*
> *As it is written, for thy sake we are killed all the day long; we accounted as sheep for slaughter.*
> *Nay, in all these things we are more than conquerors through him that loved us.*
> *For I am persuaded, that neither death, nor life, nor angels, nor principalities, nor powers, nor things present, nor things to come, nor height, nor depth, nor any other creature, shall be able to separate us from the love of God, which is in Christ Jesus our Lord.*

---

[14] James Moffat translation

Wedding, May 23, 1947

Wedding reception at home of bride's mother.

Honeymoon on a bus

Edward was twenty-nine and Rachel twenty-three as they began their life as *one* in the sight of God. They departed Durham the day after the wedding, bound for Louisville aboard a Greyhound bus. In those days, the trip was long and tedious with frequent stops along the road to pick up or let off passengers wherever they happened to want to board or disembark.

They previously had arranged to spend the weekend in Asheville, North Carolina. Arriving at the Biltmore Hotel in Asheville, long-standing reservations in hand, they were fatigued, road weary travelers. It was late at night and it had been a long, hot day on a crowded bus with standing room only. For most of the journey, Edward had stood, for it seemed every time he was able to take a seat, an elderly woman would flag down the bus and he would rise and offer her his seat. Upon presentation of their reservations, the clerk at the lobby desk advised them that because of a Lions Club convention in town, no rooms were available. Summoning an inner reserve that he was unaware he had, Edward looked the clerk coolly in the eye, brandished his reservation and demanded it be honored—a most uncharacteristic act for this quiet, non-confrontational new husband. However, he had with him his tired, lovely bride and was not to be denied! Hesitantly, the clerk found them a room.

The weekend over, they resumed their long, meandering and tiring trip, arriving in Louisville in the wee hours of the following Tuesday morning, exhausted but very happy. Unable to obtain the key to the room in which they had arranged to live in the married students' dormitory, they awoke some close friends who allowed them to collapse on the floor of their apartment. By the next day, they had the key and moved into their new home, a single room in a former men's dormitory converted to accommodate married seminary students. Their room had its own lavatory, clothes closet, double bed, study table and two chairs but the toilet and bath facilities were down the hall, one for men and one for women. Laundry facilities were in the basement. Their meals were provided in a common dining area. Nevertheless, they were together, in love and in Rachel's words, "supremely happy."

First year of marriage

Their first year of marriage was their final year at the seminary before leaving for the mission field. It was a year of rigorous, self-imposed discipline for the young couple. Rachel provided their primary financial support, working as the administrative secretary for the nursing school of Methodist Deaconess Hospital in Louisville. Utilizing her degree in religious education, she also taught a class on Christian ethics to a group of student nurses. When not at work, she spent a great deal of time typing Edward's lengthy term papers as well as helping him with his pastoral responsibilities. He took a full load of classes to complete his undergraduate seminary education, worked two part-time jobs and continued to serve as pastor of Tates Creek Baptist Church.

During this happy yet demanding year, Edward and Rachel went about the considerably time-consuming application process seeking appointment to the mission field by the Foreign Mission Board of the Southern Baptist Convention. In addition to frequent correspondence with the Board, the process entailed writing their individual detailed life history as well as elaborative summaries of their individual experience as a Christian. The process also required a systematic written account of their individual doctrinal beliefs. As essentially life-long volunteers to missions, they undertook these matters with utmost seriousness and care, for they were now at the pinnacle of their preparation for what they perceived as their divine calling.

Dreams realized

On April 6, 1948, Edward and Rachel received appointment as missionaries to Nigeria, West Africa. The official ceremony took place at the First Baptist Church in Richmond, Virginia, headquarters of the Foreign Mission Board. They traveled to Richmond by bus along with a large group of other seminary students in Louisville who had also received appointment. In Richmond, they joined groups from other seminaries who traveled there for the same purpose. Edward recorded the happy and momentous occasion in his ordination Bible:

Edward and Rachel Humphrey
Were Appointed Missionaries to
Nigeria, West Africa
April 6, 1948
By the
Foreign Mission Board
Of the
Southern Baptist Convention

Recounting the day many years later, he wrote, "Our long-held dream had been brought to realization. We were at last ready to venture upon 'the high road' of our calling. Our joy knew no bounds!"

Rachel, too, recorded her thoughts of that first year of marriage and assignment to Nigeria writing, "Even though we had so little, materially speaking, we were supremely happy. The year was filled with much prayer, with much concern as whether or not we would be accepted by the Foreign Mission Board. Our hope was fulfilled in April 1948 when we (already) commissioned by Christ, were appointed by the Southern Baptist Foreign Mission Board as missionaries to Nigeria, West Africa."

On May 7, 1948, Edward graduated from the seminary and they left Louisville headed first for North Carolina. Four weeks were spent visiting family and friends as well as packing their belongings along with supplies to last for a three-year tour of duty in Nigeria. At last, it was time to bid farewell to family members. Their first tearful parting with family took place at the home of Edward's mother in Fayetteville. His mother, Caroline, who had known longer than anyone of his heartfelt calling to foreign missions and the burdens he carried in realizing his goal, bade farewell in tears, tears of a mother's love and joy but also an expression of concern. She was not able to hide the anxiety and fear she experienced as her son went off to a distant and unknown land. As Rachel prepared to depart, her mother, Elsie, would soon be welcoming home another daughter, Doris, from Africa. John and Doris McGee were already missionaries in Nigeria and would soon be coming home on furlough. First, however, Elsie had the unusual experience of parting with Rachel, a second daughter headed for the continent of Africa. Edward and Rachel left Durham on June 11, 1948, bound for New York. Reservations were in hand to depart New York aboard *The Libreville* on June 17, 1948.

Dreams Fulfilled

He (Paul) knew love to be a reaching out to others, not with a view to gaining some personal benefit, but for the sole purpose of sharing oneself and one's possessions for the sake of anyone in need.

The Humphreys arrived in Nigeria at the time of year when the Nigerian Baptist Mission was holding its annual mission meeting. Mission meeting was a time for all of the missionaries in the Nigerian Baptist Mission to come together for a series of general meetings, committee meetings, planning, fellowship, and renewal. With the mission meeting in progress, there was no one present to extend a formal greeting or an official welcome to the newest missionaries upon their arrival. Instead, Edward and Rachel were met at their ship by a representative of the Sudan Interior Mission who gave them lodging over the weekend until missionaries of the Baptist mission returned from their meeting the following Monday. It was then that Edward and Rachel learned their initial assignment was to live and teach for a brief period in Iwo. The intention was to give them time to acclimate, adjust to a drastically different way of life and to prepare them for a more permanent assignment. After parting with their shipmate, Lavonna Lee, they waited for their loads to receive clearance by officials of the Nigerian Customs Agency and were soon on their way to Iwo in a U.S. Army jeep on loan from Rachel's sister and brother-in-law, John and Doris McGee.

Heading inland

Euphoric at the realization of their shared goal to serve God in Africa, Edward and Rachel found themselves thrust into the midst of a new and unfamiliar world. Overwhelming adjustments to a far different way of life were immediate. Edward, who had driven very little in his life, was essentially learning to drive as they very carefully began their journey inland. He had certainly never driven a vehicle with the steering wheel on the wrong side of the vehicle relative to the side of the road on which he was driving. Driving in a British colony entailed driving on the left side of the road but the jeep was by American standards with the steering wheel on the left side of the vehicle. This placed the driver in a location within the vehicle of poor visualization of oncoming traffic. That was perhaps the least of the driving difficulties he faced on this initial foray into Nigeria for he quickly discovered that very different rules of the road applied.

Driving in this new land, Edward faced a sort of baptism by fire. As they headed toward Abeokuta (ab-BEE-oh-COO-tah) where they spent the first night of a two-day journey, he immediately encountered the onslaught of speeding, untrained and usually unlicensed Nigerian drivers. Brightly painted lorries (large covered trucks) that were overflowing with passengers and all types of cargo including goats and baskets filled with chickens, barreled toward them or past them with horns blaring as if to abruptly warn, "out of the way!" The lorries seemed to follow no traffic laws. Edward very quickly discerned that one-lane bridges were best approached slowly and cautiously for otherwise it was a race to determine who could get there first!

In only a few weeks, Edward and Rachel had completed their seminary education, graduated, packed all of their belongings, bid families and friends adieu, and sailed across the Atlantic Ocean to Africa. They found themselves thrust into the Nigerian tribal and pagan culture. Confident that the hard work and accelerated pace of education to achieve appointment as missionaries was God's plan for their lives, they happily settled into their work in Iwo, ever mindful of God's grace in opening all the necessary doors to reach this pinnacle in their lives. As Edward had written over a year earlier, they were now truly on "the high road" of their calling, their "joy knew no bounds!"

Baptist College, Iwo

In Iwo, their temporary assignment was at the Baptist College, Iwo (later to become Bowen University, named after Reverend Thomas Jefferson Bowen who began Baptist mission work in Nigeria in 1850). Teaching duties began immediately while they attempted to familiarize themselves with Yoruba, the local tribal language of southwestern Nigeria. Arriving on a Friday afternoon, Edward found himself in the classroom on Monday morning, teaching subjects that were not his forte such as biology and math in addition to the more familiar courses in Bible and Christian doctrine. There was little time to adjust to the markedly different way of life on the mission field. Not only were they thrust into a diverse third world culture, but also they were busily learning the ropes as new young missionaries, adapting to a mission culture and struggling with a completely unfamiliar language. Yoruba, a melodic language, was one of the three major tribal languages spoken in Nigeria. The courses in Greek, Latin and Hebrew taken while pursuing their theological education were of little benefit in learning Yoruba.

Their new lifestyle offered few of the amenities familiar to them in their homeland. Electricity and running water were non-existent on the missionary compounds. Lighting at night was by kerosene lamps. Baths were taken only after boiling water in an outdoor wood burning hot water heater—in reality, a large iron pot set into a mound of raised earth under which was space for a wood burning fire. They learned to get along on whatever they could obtain from local markets and the occasional trip to the nearby large city of Ibadan (ee-BAD-on) where they shopped for staples. They felt well prepared by the difficult times of their youth and the financial constraints experienced while obtaining their education. To some extent, the heat and humidity of summer months spent growing up in North Carolina gave them a limited ability to cope with the heat and humidity of sub-Saharan, tropical Nigeria. But the sights and smells of many living at a subsistent level of poverty were only to be experienced, not learned beforehand.

With their love for one another well-grounded in God's love, Edward and Rachel rapidly developed a deep and abiding love for the Nigerian people. "All That I Am," took on a dual meaning, a representation that each was "all that I am" to one another as well as jointly through their ministry in missions. They were *one* in their love and *one* in their ministry. Vast cultural differences did not prevent them from forming friendships with Nigerians rapidly. Many of those friendships formed with Nigerians during the first months in Iwo remained strong, vital and loving relationships throughout their lives. At the same time, they formed enduring friendships with their fellow missionaries that lasted a lifetime. Their mission was to teach Nigerian students the curriculum in the mission schools as well as to teach Nigerians, generally, about the Gospel and the love of Christ. Toward that end, they felt strongly that their own lives should be lived in such a way as to clearly represent God's love for all humankind.

Mission culture

Adapting to the culture of the Baptist mission required learning and adjusting to the ingrained customs of a large extended family. The social life among missionaries, largely confined to those living on the same compound, was with like-minded people with a common purpose. In any given city or area of Nigeria, missionaries of the Nigerian Baptist Mission lived in homes clustered together on what was known as a compound. On larger compounds, this afforded all who lived on the compound an immediate network of friends and neighbors. On smaller ones, only one or two missionary families lived in relative isolation. In either case, all had similar goals and lifestyles as Baptist missionaries laboring in a common effort to bring Christianity to a largely pagan culture of which a significant portion of the population was of the Muslim faith.

The relatively large Nigerian Baptist mission of approximately three hundred missionaries (at its highest level) formed a relatively close-knit, loving group. When missionaries travelled within Nigeria, it was customary to schedule overnight visits with other missionaries along the way. As with any large group, friendships within the group developed more easily with some than others. A disturbing fact was that it would be many years before the missionary compounds integrated to include Nigerians. Although missionaries, in general, opposed racial segregation in the United States, the lack of integration on the compounds presented an unseemly conflict given the racial tensions that existed at the time within the United States. In later years, this practice was abolished with Nigerian faculty members and medical center personnel living with and among missionaries on the compounds.

Social gatherings among the missionaries on each compound were commonplace and frequent. Whatever the size of any given compound, the missionaries gathered regularly for prayer meetings and at the larger ones, to socialize, often for tennis, hunting or other similar sports activities. Rachel particularly enjoyed games of scrabble and tennis, but Edward did not particularly enjoy hunting, an activity enjoyed by many of his colleagues. He found it unpleasant to join in afternoon expeditions to hunt aparo—a bird akin to a guinea fowl or wild pheasant. On rare occasions, there were the hunts for bigger game, an activity he avoided entirely. He had purchased a shotgun prior to leaving North Carolina on the advice that it was almost a necessity, but soon after arrival in Nigeria, he sold it having determined that hunting did not suit his personality. On rare occasion he did find the time to enjoy a game of tennis.

Reassigned to Ede

Soon after settling into their new home in Iwo, Edward and Rachel learned that at the recent annual mission meeting, there was a decision by the personnel committee of the mission to reassign them within six months to Ede (eh-deh). Given the responsibility of opening a new Teacher Training College, Edward was to serve as its first principal. During the six months they lived in Iwo, they made numerous trips to Ede where they needed to arrange for temporary classrooms and student housing for the new school as well as to begin construction of the new college. The Baptist Mission had already appropriated funds to begin construction of permanent dormitory buildings and classroom facilities for the new college as well as a new home for its first principal. With little understanding of the language, culture and customs, and virtually no personal contacts in the area, it was a formidable task. His goal was to open the new school in January 1949 in time for the spring semester. The months passed quickly and by the end of December 1948, they moved to Ede located some 30 miles northeast of Iwo.

Baptist Teacher Training College, Ede

Ede was a small, old and historic town, its storied history traced through its provincial kings, the Timis of Ede.[15] The new college was to be located on an area of virgin land where no other buildings or any sort of infrastructure existed, recalled Benjamin Adewusi. Benjamin was one of the first students to enroll at the new college in 1949. He remembers that construction began in 1948 while the Humphreys were still residing in Iwo. Although they made frequent trips to Ede in order to supervise construction, arrange for temporary facilities and procure the necessary books and supplies required to open the new college, they encountered unnecessary delays in construction, theft of building materials and problems that came with the language barrier. In

---

[15]　Rev. Samuel Johnson, *The History of the Yorubas,* (London: Lowe & Brydone Ltd, 1969), 75-78, 155-160.

spite of these problems, Baptist Teacher Training College, Ede opened in January 1949. Classes were initially held at the First Baptist Church of Ede. It was a residential college with rooms for the students rented in the upstairs of a nearby hostel. The Foreign Mission Board assisted with books and other required teaching materials. In addition, the Humphreys contacted various churches and libraries in the United States for books and the necessary funds to insure that the first year ran smoothly. Although it was a difficult year, Benjamin, who went on to become a high school principal, says that for the college to open and operate was "evidence of God's goodness and greatness."

The Nigerians took note of Edward and Rachel's togetherness. Her unwavering encouragement and support of him in his work as the principal as well as her attendance at most of the college programs, led to her being regarded as the mother of the college, according to Benjamin Adewusi. Through the college, the Humphreys positively affected the greater Ede community as the college opening provided for many new jobs and through the jobs many new Christians. Edward and Rachel's ministry was well underway.

Home—an abandoned army barracks

The mission compound to which they moved in Ede, known as Camp Young, was a small compound with a large home adjacent to a chapel and other buildings used for retreats, conferences and various meetings. Miss Neale C. Young, a veteran missionary of many years in Nigeria, occupied the home. Camp Young had been founded with the strong spiritual and financial support of the Women's Missionary Union (WMU) of the Nigerian Baptist Convention, backed by its counterpart in the United States, the WMU affiliated with the Southern Baptist Convention. Miss Young was instrumental in the formation of the Nigerian WMU in the early 1920's and with construction of some of the early buildings on the grounds of Camp Young. Known as Aunt Nealie to Edward and Rachel, she quickly became a close and beloved mentor to the Humphreys.

In Ede, Edward and Rachel made their home in an old, abandoned army barracks on the grounds of Camp Young. The barracks, left behind by the Nigerian army, was down the hill and behind the main home in which Aunt Nealie lived. A narrow dirt path just wide enough for a single bicycle accessed the barracks. With optimism, ingenuity and determination, they set about the task of converting the barracks into their home.

The barracks itself was a three-room building constructed of weatherboard on a concrete slab. The weatherboard was painted inside and out with salignum, a black creosote-like wood preservative. Installed incorrectly, the weatherboard was upside down so that when torrential, tropical rainstorms came, water was channeled to the inside of the rooms. The slab sloped gently so that at one end, it was actually below ground level which caused water to pool inside during the heavy rains. The barracks had a tin roof, which also served as the ceiling of the rooms below. Windows were small and just above eye-level.

The barracks had no utilities, kitchen or bathroom. During early morning hours and at night, they used kerosene lamps to provide light. Kerosene was also used for refrigeration. No running water was available. Rainwater, caught in gutters along the roofline of Aunt Nealie's home was channeled into a large underground cistern, where it was stored for use in the bathroom and kitchen of her home. Water was carried by hand in buckets to the barracks from the underground cistern located near Aunt Nealie's home and stored in large fifty-five gallon drums. The water stored in drums was filtered to provide drinking water and otherwise used for cooking, bathing, and laundry.

A three-sided enclosure with a makeshift thatched roof outside the barracks served as the kitchen. The ground served as the floor of the kitchen. In the center was a mound of earth raised about two and a half feet above ground level, onto which two square-shaped empty kerosene tins were embedded with one end removed from each. The square tins served as ovens. Stretching between these two tins was a thin sheet of metal, which served as their stovetop over an open fire pit. The first torrential rainy season easily convinced them that an inside kitchen was a requirement. Using the ingenuity developed growing up on the farm in North Carolina, Edward put to good use an old-fashioned wood burning stove they brought with them from the states. A hole was cut in the sidewall of the barracks to accommodate a smoke-flue pipe and the stove was set up inside the barracks. An old-fashioned outhouse, open to the sky above served as their bathroom. Water for bathing was brought by bucket from an outdoor hot water heater similar to the type used in Iwo but located approximately one hundred and fifty yards up the hill near Aunt Nealie's home.

Rachel assumed much of the required administrative duties of the new school. In the absence of office space, she did most of the administration as well as necessary secretarial duties and bookkeeping from their bedroom at home. They approached their work at the college as a team effort and very much enjoyed this first major responsibility of their missionary career.

Most Sundays, they spent visiting and worshipping with several different churches as the associational missionary. Missionaries were assigned to various church associations of the Nigerian Baptist Convention. Each was made up of several Baptist churches in a particular area, within driving distance of the home of the assigned missionary. Acting as counselors and advisors to the various churches, the assignment required leaving home early Sunday morning, often not returning until late afternoon. Because of her pregnancy, Rachel's travel was limited and therefore she spent many of those Sundays with Aunt Nealie. Miss Young imparted valuable missionary experience to her younger counterpart as they developed a close and loving bond of friendship. To Rachel, she was a comforting and matronly individual to whom Rachel became very much attached. For as long as Aunt Nealie lived and well beyond her retirement, she kept in touch with the Humphreys and remained a part of their extended family.

An orphan becomes part of the family

A far different life story was playing out in another part of Ede. A young boy from a poverty-stricken family became an orphan forcing him to withdraw from elementary primary school for financial reasons. Joseph Ilori desperately wanted to continue in his pursuit of an education. A seemingly propitious student, he was introduced to the Humphreys as a promising young boy in need of financial assistance to continue his education. Seeing a favorable outcome all around and led through prayer, Edward and Rachel agreed to pay Joseph's school fees and purchase his textbooks and school uniform. In exchange, Joseph worked at their home helping to maintain their yard and accompanied them on their Sunday visits to various churches serving as an interpreter when Edward was asked to speak during the service. It was the beginning of a beautiful and loving relationship. Joseph became a part of the family maintaining contact with the Humphreys and their family over the ensuing years. He met and formed a friendship with their grandson, John, who in the summer of 2006 spent two months as a medical student doing research at the Baptist Medical Center, Ogbomosho.

Joseph continued his education after secondary school at the seminary in Ogbomosho. With the ongoing assistance of the Humphreys, he obtained the necessary scholarships to attend the seminary and was a student there when Edward and Rachel left Nigeria prematurely in 1965. He graduated in 1967. His excellent scholastic record and promise as a student led to sponsorship and scholarships to come to the United States where he attended East Texas Baptist University, Hardin-Simmons University and Southwestern Baptist Seminary obtaining undergraduate degrees, graduate degrees, and a divinity degree. Then, realizing the promise the Humphreys had shown in him many years earlier, in 1975, he obtained his Ph.D. from the University of North Texas whereupon he returned to Nigeria and was involved in higher education until his retirement in 2008. During that time, he enjoyed several academic appointments, culminating his career as the Dean of Academics and President of the Nigerian Baptist Theological Seminary. Following his retirement in Nigeria, in what would have pleased his "Dad and Mom in the Lord," Joseph undertook his own foreign mission to South Africa to serve as the interim principal of a seminary for one year.

Joseph had fond and loving memories of Edward and Rachel. His memories of them from 1949-1950 remained vivid and fresh as he recalled:

> *The beginning of my contact with the Humphreys, which resulted into a strong intimacy and family relationship from 1949 to around 1965 when because of the sickness of Rachel they had to leave Nigeria. I had the privilege of being close to the family. Around 1951 the Humphreys were transferred to the Nigerian Baptist Theological Seminary in Ogbomoso to serve as Seminary Lecturers. The involvement of the Humphreys in my life can be better imagined than described. The family paid all my financial expenses during my last three years in Elementary school (1949-1951). Also when I was a student at the Nigerian Baptist Theological Seminary 1954-1956, the family was also responsible for full payment of my tuition and living expenses. They were my mentors, advisors, counsellors and prayer partners. They were committed, dedicated and physically*

and spiritually involved in the success of my ministry. This was demonstrated in 1964 when I returned to the Seminary for the Bachelor of Theology degree program. The seminary faculty wrote to inform me that because I was serving as a full time Pastor, I would spend four years rather than the normal three years for the completion of the BTh degree program. I was upset and resolved to withdraw from the seminary but I shared my feeling with the Humphreys. The Humphreys counseled me and re-presented the matter to the faculty for a re-consideration of their earlier decision. He convinced the faculty of my ability to cope with the pressure of work in the church as well as that of the seminary academic work. With the intervention of Edward Humphrey, the Seminary faculty allowed me to do the BTh degree in three years. And to the glory of God, I passed all the seminary courses with distinctions and at the end of the program the seminary recommended and sponsored me for further studies in the United States just three months after the completion of my BTh in Nigeria.

The memories of my intimate association and relationship with the Humphreys, which was for about 17 years, 1949 to 1965, are still fresh as if they were yesterday. I remember the young couple moving up and down in their house as if they were brother and sister of the same parents. They were so close, so intimate and so connected that they were always together except when Edward went to work. For the remaining hours of the day throughout the week, they were together—singing hymns and choruses, praying, reading, and discussing Biblical stories, African culture, traditions or refreshing their minds of the events of their college days. It seemed to me as I watched them through the windows around their house that they were never tired of each other and that they appeared to be enjoying their time in the rural area of Nigeria where there was no television, no telephone, no cell phone, no air conditioner, and no car, except bicycle. Without having these amenities for their enjoyment, they never complained but had the joy and satisfaction of serving the Lord. They were committed to the spread of the Gospel to the Africans. Both of them were with soft-spoken voice, quiet, simple, unassuming and very reserved. Edward was a great philosopher and always applied Biblical principles in order to have a full understanding of a given situation. He was a scholar and an excellent teacher who enjoyed spending his precious time with his wife and in studying. He loved me so much and was very proud of me, my commitment to my studies and preaching ministry. He constantly expressed his great hope in my future achievements and contributions to the expansion of the gospel in Africa and beyond. He did not enjoy travelling on Nigerian roads because the roads were bad and because most of the Nigerian drivers at the time were illiterate without any respect for other road users. As a result his travelling in Nigeria was very much restricted to visiting Local Baptist Churches for occasional preaching, Baptismal Services and administration of the observance of the Lord's Supper. His regular visitors were Rev and Mrs. J.S McGee who were missionaries at Igede-Ekiti. However, Mrs. McGee was Rachel's sister. Their visit was always an occasion of great family re-union with special meals and wonderful interactions.

Remembering the Humphreys' influence on his life, Joseph wrote:

Educators believe that people:
    Learn little by what we say;
    Learn more by what we do; but
    Learn most by who we are.
    This saying describes the degree of influence of the Humphreys in my life and ministry.
    What they said, what they did and who they were greatly influenced my life. They influenced my life and ministry to become adhered to the belief that:
    Where there is faith, there is love;
    Where there is love, there is peace;
    Where there is peace, there is God;
    Where there is God, there is no need.
Their lives, commitment to mission and compassion for the needy greatly influenced me without any force or compulsion from them to seeking God's divine leadership in committing myself, gifts and opportunities to the teaching ministry and preaching passion for the lost and genuine compassion for [the] oppressed.

Remembering the Humphreys' contribution to Christian missions in Nigeria, Joseph wrote:

> *It is very impossible for any human being to have an accurate list of all the contributions or achievements of a missionary of any period in any given nation. Furthermore, we need to recognise that every missionary is only an instrument in the hand of God and as a result the glory and honour for any contributions made by a human missionary belong to God. It is only God that gives the increase and blesses the human efforts of a missionary. However, we must equally recognise the efforts and sacrifices of a servant of God, which through the grace and blessings of God have produced significant results. It may therefore be more appropriate to speak of some of the physical results of the work and missionary labour of love of Edward and Rachel Humphrey in Nigeria. The list cannot be exhaustive but only to show that their labour of love in the African mission brought forth multiple fruits. Some of the outcomes of their mission work include the following:*

> 1. *Training African leaders for tomorrow's harvest*
>   *The Humphreys had a vision and commitment to the training and preparation of the nationals (Nigerian citizens) for church ministry, for teaching ministry and for denominational leadership. The two of them were conscious of the fact that the mission work and the spread of the gospel of reconciliation in Nigeria in particular and Africa in general could be better done by Nigerians who understand the culture, the language, the value and the African ways of life. Hence, they devoted their lives, opportunities and resources to the preparation of Nigerians through teaching for the African mission. They were both involved throughout their time in Nigeria in the teaching ministry. As a result, they were privileged to have taught many of the past and present Baptist pastors, lecturers in Nigerian theological institutions, many Baptist denominational leaders and many principals and teachers of secondary schools.*

2. <u>Building and moulding the lives of Africans</u>
The Humphreys in addition to their teaching ministry integrated their faith into their daily Christian living. They used their limited personal resources to sponsor three orphans in educational institutions. They picked me up when I lost my two parents when I was just a few years old. They took care of my school expenses in elementary school as well as in the seminary. Also they sponsored Morakinyo Taiwo throughout his years in the Nigerian Baptist Seminary, Ogbomoso. Taiwo graduated from the seminary and served as pastor of many different Baptist churches in Nigeria. He was used of God to lead many souls to Christ. Now he has died to be with his Lord. I had the privilege to preach at his funeral. The third orphan that was picked and helped through his education was Ishola, the son to the Humphreys' cook. He was trained to become a schoolteacher and he had the privilege of teaching many Nigerian children. The Humphreys were given the grace to assist the three of us (Joseph, Taiwo and Ishola) to have a meaningful experience in life. The Humphreys helped the three of us to know Christ and to accept Jesus Christ into our lives. To God be the glory.

3. <u>Restoration of broken relationships.</u>
Edward Humphrey during his missionary years in Nigeria served in adding to his teaching ministry, as a missionary adviser to many Baptist churches in Nigeria. He used to visit these churches on Sundays, preached and stayed after service to settle misunderstandings, conflicts and clashes between the pastor and the church. He exercised patience, maturity, godliness and meekness in patiently listening to the various complaints and then offered advice and reconciliation. Sometimes he would miss his lunch and dinner. He never complained but counted it a privilege to serve as God's instrument in bringing peace into the church of Christ. Since he could not speak any of the Nigerian languages, he used to take me along to these churches as his interpreter. I enjoyed being with him and being around a white man gave me an

unimaginable recognition, respect and acceptance among my fellow Nigerians. At the time, not many Africans had the privilege of being close to and travelling with a white man. The Humphreys assisted me to have hope, to anticipate a better future and to work hard to meet people's and God's expectations.

Conclusion:
This list of contributions of the Humphreys is by no means exhaustive but these are just a few of them.

Joseph Ilori, 2010

Godly love

Before the birth of her first child, Rachel occasionally accompanied Edward on his Sunday trips to the various churches within his assigned association as the associational missionary. It was on one such Sunday that she more fully understood the prophetic words she had inscribed within his wedding band. They were words that not only applied to their love for one another but also to their love as extended through their ministry in His service. On a trip one Sunday morning to a church near Ire (EE-ray), a town not far from Ede, they happened upon a man lying in the middle of the road. Whether delirious from an accident they had not witnessed or mentally ill, the man was clearly injured, filthy and needed attention, the least of which was to remove him from the danger of lying in the middle of the road. Many years later, Rachel vividly recalled the scene as Edward stopped the jeep and without hesitation went over to assist the man. Deeply moved, she watched as he cradled the stranger's squalid, mud-encrusted head in his lap, gave him water and tended to his wounds. Together they were able to place him in the back seat of the jeep and take him on to Ire where the Baptist mission compound had a small clinic staffed by a missionary nurse. Continuing on to the church they were visiting that Sunday, Rachel realized more than ever they were *one* in their ministry to the Nigerian people. She had been witness to godly love as evidenced by Edward's response to the stranger lying in the road. Decades later, in his book entitled *The Form of Godliness,* Edward described godly love as, "Godly love, like faith...encompasses the whole of life... Human love is what it is first of all before God and unto God, and therefore it is primarily the response of obedience to its Lord. But it has its whole existence in relation to one's fellow-men, and therefore it is what it is, and all that it is, in response to actual human situations."

Then there were three

Dr. Gilliland had advised Rachel early in her pregnancy to be prepared to come to Ogbomosho to stay for the final month prior to the delivery of her baby. Edward drove back and forth between Ede and Ogbomosho on the weekends during February of 1949. On March 4, 1949, their first child, a son, was born—the most precious of gifts bestowed by God upon a couple so deeply in love, the gift of a new life. March 4 was also the birthday of Caroline, Edward's mother, and quite fittingly, they named their new son for Caroline's husband and Edward's father, Stinson. Their excitement and joy was cause for Dr. Gilliland to remark to another missionary, "They acted like Stinson was the first baby ever to be born."

As was customary of the times, Rachel was required to spend two additional weeks in Ogbomosho with her new baby to be near her doctors. Physicians felt it necessary for both mother and child to be under direct supervision for an extended period when in the tropics and more so when living in a relatively remote area of a third world country. Edward continued the weekend commute between Ede and

Ogbomosho until the time came when he was able to bring Rachel and Stinson home to Ede. During this time, Rachel wrote letters to Edward from "Stinson and Rachel" and Edward wrote to "My Darling Wife and My Precious Little Boy." When the time came, Edward and Rachel brought Stinson back home to the army barracks. During this time, Rachel discovered she had adjusted remarkably well to Africa and their new lifestyle. During the day, Edward was teaching at the college and therefore she was on her on with her new infant son. The upside down weatherboard was sorely inadequate in preventing flooding inside the barracks when the tropical rainstorms came. Fortunately, water collected at the end of the house below ground level, enabling Rachel to keep the baby's crib on dry ground. When the occasional poisonous tropical snake found its way inside, she discovered she quickly mastered the ability to decapitate it with a garden hoe, much to her surprise. Nevertheless, it was a joyous and happy time. They were grateful, filled with love for each other, for their son and for their ministry among the Nigerian people.

Stinson with Aunt Nealie Young, 1949

Rachel, 1950

Edward and Stinson, 1949

Edward and Stinson, 1950

Rachel and Stinson, 1950

Edward, Stinson and Rachel, 1950

Family traditions

John and Doris McGee returned to Nigeria from their furlough in the summer of 1949. Edward had never met the McGees until then. Although stationed in a different part of the country, they were close enough to visit frequently. Rachel and her older sister, Doris, grew closer while Edward and John developed a relationship very much like brothers. Both families felt fortunate to have immediate family members within the same country overseas. Committed to the common cause of missions, the two couples drew on close familial bonds as they developed enduring and loving relationships.

The McGees, who had purchased a new automobile while on furlough, needed help driving it to their home in Igede (EE-ged-EE). Edward drove the jeep, which the Humphreys had used during the previous year, while John, together with the two young families, drove their new Chevrolet. A family holiday tradition began at Christmas of that year and continued throughout their service in Nigeria. The two families began a rotation of spending most significant holidays, including Christmas, at one of their homes, together as extended family. Christmas 1949 was spent in Igede where the McGees were assigned. The following Christmas, the McGee family joined the Humphreys in Ede. Every year the two families were together at Christmas with the exception of years when one family was on furlough. It was a special time for both families. Over time, the children of both families grew to establish relationships closer than that of cousins; theirs would become more nearly that of siblings.

Ministry accomplished in Ede

A great deal was accomplished during the eighteen months the Humphreys spent in Ede. Edward and Rachel continued their teaching and administrative duties at the college in Ede through December 1950. When they left at the conclusion of the fall semester, they were able to turn over administration of the college to a Nigerian principal. Writing about their time in Ede, Rachel entered in her diary: "The road was not easy and we made mistakes, for there were new people, new culture, new language, new educational system—all to learn."

Edward's work with churches within his assigned association continued and a special relationship developed in this capacity with a small church serving the needs of a colony of lepers. The small leper colony located approximately two miles from their home had within its confines a small church. It was in that small church that Edward began every Sunday morning, worshipping with the unfortunate souls relegated to living at the colony. From there, he visited several other churches each Sunday before returning home in the late afternoon. His attendance at that small church had one of the greatest impacts on him. In 1949, he wrote a brief narrative entitled "The Lepers' Mite" which serves as an example of the Humphreys' fond attachment to the Nigerian people.

It was Sunday morning in the little clan settlement near Ede, Nigeria. The multitude of the maimed and the halt were answering the summons to worship. Across the valley, two miles away, and situated on the highest hill in town was the Baptist Church of Ede. But for these poor unfortunate creatures, that sanctuary was a forbidden place, for they were "unclean."

Through the midst of the intervening valley flowed the waters of the Oshun River, the chief water supply of the town. But even the right to be baptized was denied these folk, for they were "unclean." In the town, were those whose ministries might have lifted untold burdens from the hearts of these wretched ones— might have, but they were afraid, for these were "unclean."

Dwelling in isolation, apart from the rest of mankind, and "unclean", this little company of more than sixty souls was assembling for worship. Their own little church building, which had been provided by the Baptist Mission of Nigeria, stood on an elevation over-looking the camp. Up the incline they filed, some plodding wearily, and no doubt painfully. There were the five little boys who always sit in the front row. There was also the little girl whose lovely face portrays the sweet innocence of childhood. There was the old woman ("Iya"—mother as she was called), whose leg seemed to swell more and more from week to week, and whose step was becoming noticeably heavy. And there was the crippled old man ("Baba" as he was called), who it seems to me, is without question one of the choicest of the saints of God. There was a mother with an infant in her arms. There were youth and middle-aged and aged folk. These dear ones moved quietly and reverently down the aisle and into the pews until the assembly was complete.

The service had not seemed different than usual that day. There was the usual period of prayer and praise, followed by a message of the spoken word. There was more singing, and then it was time for the benediction. At that point, one of the men stepped out of his pew and into the aisle. He spoke feelingly of the fact that this little band of believers had themselves received the gospel by means of the gifts of others. And then he related that these folk had themselves become convinced through Bible study that they ought to contribute something toward the proclamation of the gospel. He said that they had decided that they would make the giving of an offering a part of their worship of God. This spontaneous and wholly unexpected response on the part of these poor folk came as a surprise to me, the preacher. But an offering was received that day. It consisted mainly of coins, each worth one-tenth of an English penny. These votive offerings from the "unclean" outcasts of society were bathed in a cleansing agent to render them acceptable and were then sent on to the Baptist headquarters for use in its mission outreach.

I went home that day pondering in the depths of my soul a beautiful incidence of the power of the gospel. Here they were, the objects in turn of the deepest sympathy and of the saddest neglect of mankind. Yet, deep within these simple outcasts there had been born the sense of a debt of love and godly duty, which had now led to an open act of consecration. I asked myself that day: "Can anyone hear ever so faintly above the response of his own soul that age-old cry, "Unclean, unclean"? And I wondered what miserly soul could clasp in his hand that which should match these gifts.

I fancy that One stood hard-by the heavenly treasury that day, "and He looked up and saw the rich men casting their gifts into the treasury. And He saw also certain poor lepers casting in thither their mites. And He said, 'Of a truth I say unto you that these poor lepers have cast in more than they all: for all these have of their abundance cast in unto the offerings of God: but these lepers have of their want cast in all they had."

This had been a day of rest. Crippled limbs had relaxed from the daily toil of eking out a meager living from their assigned plots of ground. Lonely hearts had forgot for a time their sorrows. Poverty had given way to joy in their Lord. In the midst of pain and suffering, hope had been renewed and peace had reigned supreme. The call to worship had come like the glad peal of the dawn. There was nothing majestic about these simple folk, save their humble reverence—nothing of the stately dignity, save their simple faith. But hallowed by the glory (i.e. the presence) of God, here was indeed a "colony of heaven!"

Family expansion

During the years Edward and Rachel lived in Ede, Stinson grew into a toddler, doted on by Aunt Nealie Young. He became a big brother on December 3, 1950, when a sister, Neale Susan (named for both her great grandfather, Neill and Aunt Nealie) was born. The same effusive excitement experienced at Stinson's birth took place at Susan's birth. By this time, they had moved into a new home built for the principal of the Teacher Training College in Ede. However, preparations were soon underway for the family to move to Ogbomosho.

Describing the births of her two children in a summary of their first tour, Rachel wrote, "I cannot fail to mention two highlights of our first tour. The first happened on March 4, 1949 when Stinson Edward came into our home. We were thrilled beyond words. Then the night of December 3, 1950, Neale Susan was born. Our joy was equally full when she came. Our children have been a constant joy to us here on the mission field, and we feel that God has blessed us richly in them."

Seminary teaching career

As the fall semester of 1950 ended in Ede, it was time for the Humphreys to begin a long overdue formal study of the Yoruba language. Yoruba was the primary tribal language spoken in southwestern Nigeria. In January 1951, the mission transferred the Humphrey family to Ogbomosho. During what was to be a six-month study of Yoruba, they struggled to learn the melodic, tonal language. However, as Rachel later wrote, "For three months we struggled with a tonal language. I might say that even now, we do not know the language as we would like to know it." What was to be a six-month term of language study was cut short to three months when one of the professors at the Nigerian Baptist Theological Seminary in Ogbomosho was unexpectedly forced to return to the United States for family health reasons. The mission turned to Edward to take his place on the faculty. Rachel wrote, "Edward was privileged to teach at the seminary our last three months of our first tour."

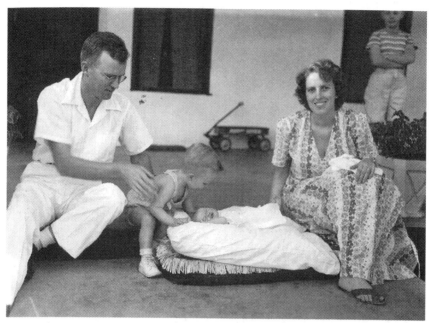

(L to R) Edward, Stinson, Susan, and Rachel,
just after Susan's birth, December 3, 1950

The "old" (original) Seminary building.

In her account of the last six months of their first tour in Nigeria, Rachel wrote, "We now moved into one of the large, two story homes on the seminary compound and Edward began teaching church history to the seminary students. It was a work he loved and had long hoped that he might be permitted to fulfill his calling to missions in just this way." They were now in a much more spacious living situation, with indoor utilities and on a large compound that housed numerous missionaries, some of whom served on the seminary faculty and some in various roles at the Baptist Medical Center. Their new home was adjacent to the seminary itself. It was a dramatic change for the young family. The children now had playmates, many of whom would remain their friends into adulthood.

Edward thrived in his new role as a professor teaching church history. The Nigerian Baptist Theological Seminary was the highest academic level of theological institutions in West Africa at the time. He had arrived in Nigeria willing for God to lead the way, willing to accept any assignment, yet hoping to serve in this capacity if such an opportunity occurred.

First tour completed

Missionaries to West Africa customarily spent a tour of three years on the mission field followed by approximately twelve months on furlough in the United States. A tour followed by a furlough was customary during that period of time, a practice now changed with the advent of jet air travel and the need to provide a wider range of alternatives to attract people willing to serve as missionaries.

In July 1951, the Humphrey family departed Nigeria for their first yearlong furlough in the United States. In what seemed like a quick trip at the time, they flew by prop plane over the Sahara desert to Tripoli, Libya. Mechanical difficulties forced an overnight stay in the airport in Tripoli. Feeling they could not leave the airport in the event the plane was repaired and with little in the way of eating facilities, a miserable night was spent in the dilapidated terminal. It was then on to London, New York and home to North Carolina and joyful reunions with families who had never met Stinson and Susan. Siblings of both Edward and Rachel were at Raleigh-Durham International Airport to greet the young family. Their two mothers, Caroline and Elsie, waited at their respective homes for their reunion and the joy of embracing two new grandchildren. Caroline,

Edward's mother, seemed especially joyful in a letter written just three weeks before her reunion with the young family.

Furlough

The Humphreys began their furlough spending a few weeks visiting family they had not seen in three years. Both Edward and Rachel, who had grown up in large, close-knit families had maintained close contact with their families throughout their first tour in Nigeria. Although they exchanged frequent letters, the families wanted to hear the details first-hand. They spent a few days in the homes of each of their siblings as well as more lengthy visits with their two mothers. It was a special time of loving family reunion. Missionaries on furlough usually spent the year near their families. The year was not a year of vacation but rather a working year with obligations to spend several weeks in what were termed "schools of missions" in various parts of the country. These were weeklong meetings at various churches within an association of churches belonging to the Southern Baptist Convention. Various missionaries from countries around the world gathered for these schools, speaking, telling about their mission work and experiences on the mission field, often meeting in small groups with people particularly interested in the country in which they served. These weeks usually required extensive travel, at times to distant states.

In addition to the schools of missions, missionaries spent many of their weekends traveling to nearby towns and cities. On Sunday morning, they were the featured speaker at the Sunday morning worship service, followed by an afternoon of visiting with interested church members, and concluding the day or weekend with a Sunday evening audio-visual presentation depicting their work in the country of their assignment.

The Humphreys spent most of the first furlough at the seminary in Louisville rather than living near family. They moved into the missionary apartments at the seminary and Edward began further post-graduate study that would eventually lead to a doctoral degree in theology. This was the first year of what would ultimately prove to be a ten year quest for his doctorate. With only one year out of every four spent in formal study at the seminary in Louisville, it was a long and arduous road. As he had during his college career, he undertook the heaviest academic load possible to accomplish his goal of obtaining his doctorate in as short a time as possible. While taking required classes, he also began the necessary research for his doctoral thesis. The library at Southern Baptist Theological Seminary provided him the necessary resources for his research. Once this furlough year was over, it would be another three years before he could avail himself of the necessary types of research materials.

Illness and unexpected family loss

In December 1951, the family suffered three unexpected times of grief-stricken sadness and concern. Just three days apart, Edward's mother died of a heart attack and Rachel's brother-in-law died of a similar cause. What was to be a quick trip to North Carolina for the funerals became complicated and extended when their daughter, Susan, was hospitalized by a serious and life threatening illness. Susan's illness, which was never diagnosed, was of such severe nature that she required hospitalization during the time the family was in North Carolina for the funerals. When it was thought Susan might not survive, Rachel regretfully felt she could not attend Caroline's funeral thus foregoing the ability to support Edward at an important emotional time in his life, a circumstance that was very disturbing to her. Caroline's death at fifty-seven years of age had come as a traumatic shock for Edward who attended her funeral with his son, Stinson. The memory of his grandmother's funeral would stand as one of Stinson's earliest memories.

Study, rest, and rejuvenation

The remainder of the furlough proceeded uneventfully with the exception of Susan's slow recovery from the undiagnosed illness. During the time she was hospitalized, she essentially lost the ability to walk and bravely set about the task of regaining that ability.

Along with his classes and research, Edward was involved with several schools of missions and other speaking engagements. Otherwise, the family enjoyed a taste of American life, made new friends and visited with many old friends from seminary days. The children discovered delicious novelties such as real mayonnaise as opposed to homemade, whole milk as opposed to powdered milk and whole bread that to them tasted like cake. The family enjoyed the spring of 1952 and in May, Edward and Rachel celebrated their fifth anniversary. As was his custom, he wrote her an anniversary letter of love. Soon after, they prepared to leave for North Carolina and another round of visiting both sides of their respective families before leaving for Nigeria.

Edward, Stinson and Susan on furlough in Louisville, 1952

Susan learning to walk again after life threatening illness, 1952

Humphrey Family, 1952

Our Fifth Anniversary
May 23, 1952

My Darling Rachel,

These five years have brought a world of sweetness into my life. The confidence and trust which you continually inspire within me becomes more sacred with the passing years. Your ideal, ever-present sweetheart love burns its way ever more deeply into my very being, and thereby awakens a charm and wonder too deep-seated for utterance. Your steadfast loyalty to our avowed purpose of service in bringing to a lost world the glorious Gospel of the Son of Righteousness continues to be a joy to me. And darling, we are so dependent upon each others faithfulness at that point!

In the blessed experience of parenthood you have been the ideal mother to our children, proving yourself completely worthy of the name.

I thank God for you, Rachel, and pray that I may prove in some measure worthy of your love.

All of my love always,

Edward

Fifth anniversary letter, Edward to Rachel, May 23, 1952

97

Return to Nigeria

In July 1952, after visiting with family members in North Carolina, the Humphrey family departed from New York once again aboard ship, bound first for Great Britain, then on to Lagos. In New York, before departing, they took ownership of their very first automobile. The two-tone, lime green and white 1953 Chevrolet was the most expensive purchase of their lives to date. They felt an automobile had become a necessity to carry out their mission work. The car went with them as cargo aboard the passenger ship *R.M.S. Britannic* of the Cunard Steamship Company.

This voyage was considerably more upscale when compared to *The Libreville,* the freighter they had traveled aboard in 1948. Not only did they have two children along but also the passenger ship was luxurious compared to the austere freighter taken on their first voyage. This time they sailed with the certainty of love for a land and people they already knew. They were anxious to return. Rachel wrote, "This time, we knew the people to whom we were going, and we loved them. We knew something of their background and culture and accepted it. We knew that we were going to our home, and we looked forward to it. We were going to an unfinished task, and we were grateful for the privilege."

The ship, a British vessel with British customs, required that children spend most of the day separated from parents. Formal meals for the adults were served at a separate time and place than that of the children. For the first time, Rachel experienced consternation and concern that accompanied extended periods of separation from her children. In Nigeria, the children led a cloistered life, limited to the compound in Ogbomosho. Rachel had never spent any time of forced separation from her children and readily voiced her dismay to no avail.

Upon arrival in Lagos, they were pleased to learn the Mission had reassigned them to serve at the seminary in Ogbomosho. That had been their desire all along; indeed, it was the primary motivation for Edward to begin his graduate study while on furlough. He felt more at home in a seminary setting than in a teacher training college. The seminary would be the center of their service for the remainder of their missionary career.

Life on the Mission Field

Genuine Christian obedience has its own law, which conforms to love rather than to logic. It is a human response, arising out of the heart, or not at all.

Arrival in Lagos in August 1952 was a far different experience for the Humphreys compared to their first arrival in 1948. On this occasion, a representative of the Mission met the family as they disembarked. The family stayed at the mission guesthouse in Lagos for a few days waiting for the off-loading of the new Chevrolet and their loads. They then drove to Ogbomosho, now only a one-day trip inland with more direct routes and major improvements in road condition. Their loads would follow by lorry. They were more familiar with the country, with the people and with driving on the left side of the road. It was an exciting trip. They were thrilled to be going back to the same home on the seminary compound in Ogbomosho that they had left a year earlier and Edward was to be a permanent, full-time member of the faculty at the seminary. Of this permanent assignment to Ogbomosho, Rachel wrote, "We had hoped that someday we would be permitted to do this type of work; therefore, we were happy when we learned of the transfer." In a statement reflecting her trust in God, Rachel continued by writing, "What the future holds for us, we do not know. We are willing to be shown, one step at a time." It would not be the last time she expressed her faith in this way.

Life in the big house

The family moved into the same large, old two-story home in which they had lived at the conclusion of their first tour. The building itself was a thick-walled mud structure with wide, open verandas on both levels that reached around almost three quarters of the building. It was a spacious home with large, high ceilinged rooms. The main level consisted of a kitchen, dining room, living room and large storage areas. Bedrooms were on the second level. This home had indoor bathrooms with running water. Rainwater, collected by gutters, was stored in a large underground cistern. A gasoline pump was used to pump the water to an overhead holding tank from which running water was supplied to the house using gravity flow. Electricity was not yet available; therefore, kerosene was the energy source for lighting and refrigeration.

Stinson and Susan remembered this as their first childhood home. It was near the site missionary children gathered to play, attend school during the week and Sunday school before going to church on Sundays. They formed lifelong relationships during this time that generated many fond memories and would remain an important aspect of their lives. The home had a large surrounding yard in which Edward hung swings and placed playground structures he built for the children. Compared to the barracks in Ede, this was the first home that Rachel felt was a suitable home in which to raise a family. Originally built for the president of the seminary, it was one of the larger homes on the compound in spite of its age.

The Humphreys' home, just inside the front entrance of the seminary compound, was adjacent to the seminary itself. A large complex of new buildings was under construction nearby. Construction of the new seminary was completed in 1955. A dedication plaque located just outside the library listed among others, the names of Rev. and Mrs. J.E. Humphrey.

Nigerian Baptist Theological Seminary, Ogbomosho

The Ogbomosho Baptist mission compound was the largest in Nigeria in terms of size and number of missionaries. It was a large compound with two major institutions. The seminary and its associated buildings were on the southern portion of the compound and included housing for missionaries assigned to the seminary in one capacity or another, as well as housing and dining facilities for the seminary students. On the northern portion of the compound was the Baptist Medical Center, which included the hospital, nursing school and housing for missionaries assigned in one capacity or another to the medical center. In addition to the large primary compound, a smaller compound with a leprosy center was a few miles away, just outside of town. Housing for missionaries who worked there was on that smaller compound, its location outside of town because of the age-old stigma associated with leprosy.

Missionaries stationed in Ogbomosho lived in what was much like a small American community or neighborhood, the primary difference being that all that lived there were in some way involved with Baptist mission work in Nigeria. Because of the availability of medical care at the medical center, the seminary library, and the availability of large housing and dining facilities located at the seminary, most of the Baptist missionaries in Nigeria visited Ogbomosho on an annual basis and often more frequently. Missionaries who lived in Ogbomosho regularly opened their homes to others who visited. Many other Americans and expatriates from various countries residing within Nigeria visited as well, primarily for medical care. Upon completion of the new facilities at the seminary in 1955, Ogbomosho became the site of the annual meeting of the entire mission. The seminary offered a variety of suitable meeting rooms, a large auditorium and a dining facility. These facilities together with the missionary homes on the compound met the needs required to house and hold meetings of over two hundred people and their children.

Missionary responsibilities

Edward's primary responsibility was as a faculty member and professor of church history at the Nigerian Baptist Theological Seminary. As such, the courses he taught were primarily in church history but depending on the faculty member on furlough, he taught other courses across the spectrum of theological education. These included courses in systematic theology, theology, and philosophy. He approached the courses he taught in a very serious manner, spending long hours in preparation for each class. He was steadfast in his determination that his students deserved his best efforts; thus his preparation, he felt, should be at the highest level he was capable of providing. He never felt he was over-prepared. Writing about Edward as his professor, Joseph Ilori wrote:

> I had the privilege of being his student and studied the fore mentioned courses under him. I did not want to disappoint him hence I had to spend several hours in preparation for his classes.
>
> He loved me so much and was very proud of me, my commitment to my studies and preaching ministry. He constantly expressed his great hope in my future achievements and contributions to the expansion of the gospel in Africa and beyond.

Edward also served as associational missionary to the Ogbomosho North Association. That association contained all the churches and preaching points in and around Ogbomosho and north to the Niger River. This required that he travel extensively on most Sundays to the various churches within that association. On most Sundays, the family stayed in Ogbomosho to attend church at Eastern Antioch Baptist Church, but on many Sundays, Stinson accompanied his father to the churches he visited. It was a special time they both enjoyed, a time of sharing and of love. Stinson learned much about the spectrum of life on these trips to as many as four churches on any given Sunday. They usually attended two services before sharing a picnic lunch on a dirt road a few miles from nowhere and then often drove on to another church meeting. Then, embraced in the security of a nap taken with his head laid on his father's lap, they journeyed home.

Self-imposed responsibilities

Throughout the second and third tours of service, Edward spent most evenings in his office at the seminary. He studied late into the night and on weekends, preparing for and writing the dissertation required to obtain his doctoral degree in theology. He took the required written examinations while on furlough in Louisville in 1955-56. The long hours spent away from home in pursuit of his doctorate always concerned him. For the remainder of his life, he frequently spoke about it as means of explaining what he perceived as his lack of involvement in family life. He expressed anxiety over the degree to which he felt torn between the needs of his family and the efforts required to obtain his doctorate. He felt an obligation to the seminary and its students to obtain the degree and, in fact, it was a major factor in maintaining the necessary institutional academic accreditation. The level of anxiety he felt was born of his love of family and love of service to his calling. It was his anxiety alone and not one shared by Rachel or his family. Always supportive of his efforts, she had inscribed "All That I Am" within his wedding ring. It was a commitment she made to him at the time of their marriage and forever thereafter.

The many roles of a missionary wife

As was the custom of most missionary wives during this era, Rachel's primary duty was to support and care for her family. There were many other activities and responsibilities but her role as wife and mother came first. Edward was supportive of the way in which she prioritized her responsibilities. She supported her family by assuming responsibility for their day-to-day needs. She was a very involved mother and enjoyed every aspect of her children's lives. As her own mother had done, she sewed essentially all of her children's clothes. It was not only practical but also economical.

Along with other mothers on the compound, she helped set up a small school for the missionary children that began in kindergarten and went through the fourth grade. That there were enough children on one compound to form a school was an advantage not enjoyed by many of the missionary families scattered around the country in more remote areas and on compounds that were more isolated. Rachel, along with other missionary wives served as schoolteachers. The curriculum they used as their resource was the Calvert Home School curriculum (based in Baltimore, Maryland). The same curriculum was used when the children went to boarding school. Edward participated by teaching a class in Greek mythology. He had minored in Greek when at Wake Forest and enjoyed this special time with his young students. In the evenings, Rachel was the parent who played games and read bedtime stories with the children.

Rachel nurtured her children's spiritual as well as physical needs. Susan recalled one particular conversation with her mother as a young girl. Rachel was talking about seeing people from biblical times when she got to heaven, causing Susan to ask her, "When we get to heaven, will you hold me up so I can see Jesus?" Rachel replied, "I'm trying to do that right now."

In addition to the responsibilities of home and family, Rachel began teaching a class on the Bible each morning to boys and girls at a nearby primary day school. She also began teaching in the women's division of the seminary. Her students were the wives of seminary students. The classes she taught were primarily in home economics, religious education and teaching the wives of seminary students about their roles as future pastors' wives. She also led devotional services at the hospital, tutored at the school for the blind and organized a volunteer band of seminary students to conduct street services in Ogbomosho.

During the second tour, Rachel assumed the duties of bookkeeper for the leprosy center. The center was not only a treatment facility with an assigned physician and nurse, but was also a collection of villages in which people with leprosy or the deformities that resulted from the disease lived along with their families. Those unfortunate to have had leprosy were ostracized by society. Many of the children living at the center did not have leprosy but lived with their parents until old enough to integrate into society. It was a large settlement with small individual villages scattered about. Each was a small community within a larger community of lepers. Rachel kept the financial records for the entire center for the duration of her mission service in Nigeria. Her time spent at the leprosy center was also a time the children enjoyed for it was a small compound of its own that housed a missionary family with several children similar in age to Stinson and Susan. The weekly trips to the center meant an afternoon of playing with friends. Particularly enjoyable was a large reservoir where they played and fished. People with leprosy were not allowed to share a reservoir with the general population, another form of isolation they endured.

A small room between the house and garage at the Humphrey home became a barbershop of sorts. Once every two weeks, Rachel served as the barber for the men and boys living on the compound in Ogbomosho. Many of the missionaries had special skills they shared and cutting hair was one of hers. She very much enjoyed the extra time of one on one visiting with all who came regularly for haircuts. A few years later she took her barbershop to Newton Memorial School, the boarding school the children would all attend, going twice a month to give the boys haircuts. This also gave her, as well as Edward, an afternoon to spend time with their children who were students at Newton. Rachel's life was full and with her vigorous, vivacious manner, she exuded her love of family, friends and work. It was readily apparent that Rachel was happy and content in her work.

Nigerian employees

Nigerians hired to help them around their home allowed the Humphreys to keep their busy schedules. Jobs for Nigerians were scarce and those offered by the missionaries were highly sought after for those jobs gave them a certain amount of financial security that was otherwise unavailable. These jobs created a situation that benefited all involved. The extreme poverty of most Nigerians provided only a subsistence living. Jobs offered by the missionaries were among the highest paying available. The level of poverty among Nigerians was so desperate that a missionary family could afford to employ several people on what was a relatively low salary by American standards. Rachel employed Ishola as a cook and steward. Ojo was the laundry man who washed and ironed clothes and linens. Isaiah was the gardener who kept a large and bountiful vegetable garden and fruit trees providing food year around. These three young men were trusted and valuable employees who in reality became a part of the family. To the children, they were friends whose company they enjoyed. These men worked for the Humphreys loyally throughout their time in Nigeria.

Edward and Rachel hired seminary students on a part-time basis for help with care of and looking after the children. In addition, they assumed financial responsibility for some of these students' school fees, textbooks, uniforms and often a portion of their living expenses. Many of these students became extended members of the family and remained as such throughout their lives. Two of these students were orphans whose lives dramatically changed after becoming acquainted with the Humphreys, in effect, becoming their surrogate parents. Joseph Ilori thrived in his education at all levels, eventually became a seminary student and ultimately President of the Nigerian Baptist Theological Seminary. Morakinyo Taiwo served as Stinson's babysitter beginning in 1950 and maintained a life-long loving relationship with the Humphrey family. He became the pastor of a Baptist church in the Ekiti district (Ondo State) of Nigeria, near Igede where the McGees lived. The last visit with Taiwo occurred in 1990 when Stinson visited Ogbomosho on a medical mission trip to work in the hospital in which he was born. While there, Taiwo traveled four hours by lorry to visit him, a time of joyful reunion. Over the years, these two students continued the familial relationships formed in prior decades through regular written contact with the family.

Many facets of missionary life

Edward and Rachel brought certain skills and experience learned earlier in life to the mission field. Edward became an expert mechanic while working on the farm and at Glenn Martin Aircraft Company. He put that training and experience to good use during the second tour when a large generator arrived in Ogbomosho to provide electricity to the various buildings on the compound. When assembled, it would provide electricity for an hour in the early morning and a few hours each evening. However, it arrived in small pieces within large crates and required meticulous assembly. In a small building, later called the light plant, several of the missionary men, including Edward, set about the task of unpacking all the parts and assembling the generator. It took several weeks and considerable team effort. Once assembled and functional, the large generator had the capacity to supply electricity to all the buildings on the entire compound.

The light plant also had an area set aside for the necessary servicing and mechanical repairs of automobiles. A car in need of any type of mechanical maintenance or repair could be driven inside the building and over a large pit into which one could descend stairs to access the undercarriage of the car. Edward willingly shared his abilities with other missionary families who needed their cars serviced. Beginning at about eight years of age, Stinson enjoyed this special time with his father who, over time, used it to pass on valuable knowledge and skills. Edward also used the trips back and forth from home to the light plant to teach his son how to drive. Most importantly, the time together was spent discussing a broad range of topics that would engender wonderful memories of an enduring father-son relationship.

Essentially all of the Humphreys' furniture was mahogany furniture Edward masterfully designed and built over the years. He purchased the necessary tools and enjoyed the work, but above all, the construction of nearly all of their furniture was an expression of love for his darling. Designed to match a style Rachel picked from pictures in a Sears and Roebuck catalog, it was truly a labor of love. He enjoyed the break from his work on his doctorate and was proud of the pieces he produced. More important to him was Rachel's delight in his pieces of furniture. She was always eager to tell friends and visitors from where it came.

The Nigerian people often called upon missionaries for varied reasons and at various times of the day. It was not unusual for someone to knock on the door at any time of day or night seeking transportation for a variety of reasons. It could be for a mother in labor ("Madonna and child" as Edward termed it) or a person in an outlying village with an injury requiring medical attention. At times, a student simply needed a ride to his home village to tend to the needs of his family. Edward never turned down the messenger, often gone for hours on his mission of mercy or kindness. Perhaps more frequently, Rachel tended to all manner of minor cuts, scrapes and injuries of strangers passing by her home to or from their farms in the outlying countryside. She helped those she could or made certain those in need received adequate help at the nearby medical center. With the heart of servants, Edward and Rachel undertook their service to the Nigerian people.

Family Life

Edward and Rachel provided a nurturing and loving home for their children. They strived to pass on the values instilled in them by their own parents and grandparents. On September 19, 1953 Edna Rachel was born, the third and last child born into the Humphrey family. At the suggestion of Edna Goldie, a fellow missionary and the wife of the physician assigned to the leprosy center, she was named to honor the given names of her parents. She was also born at Frances Jones Memorial Nursing Home. Once again, Edward and Rachel expressed effusive excitement, rejoicing in the expansion of their love. Stinson and Susan joined in the celebration of a new sibling, while asking for more. Edna Rachel's first home was the two-story home near the old seminary building. The Humphreys resided in that home throughout their second tour, leaving it when they went on furlough in the summer of 1955.

A typical day in the life of the Humphrey family during this time began with family breakfast followed by each going off to whatever activity they were involved in that day whether it was teaching, bookkeeping, school or play. The family gathered again for the noontime meal, followed by a rest period. The parents took brief naps while the children either napped or enjoyed some quiet activity in their own room. Most missionary families followed this pattern of early afternoon quiet times as most felt it was necessary when living in the tropics. For the children, afternoons were for playing or going into town with their mother. The family again gathered for the evening meal followed by a time of family devotion. Devotional time was a time for reading a devotional story, Bible study and prayer. Family devotional time always concluded with a time in which each family member from youngest to oldest prayed aloud. It was a time in which the children learned to pray. But it was also a time that generated humorous memories. Prayers, particularly those of their parents that seemed interminably long to young children with short attention spans, elicited varied responses from each of them. Edna Rachel, the youngest, often fell asleep in her mother's lap while Stinson attempted, sometimes successfully, to engage Susan in games of tic-tac-toe played with their fingers on Edward's back. Their father never complained and for the rest of their lives, this special family time would remain a fond memory for each of them, particularly as a daily special family time. The devotional time was not only important to the manner in which Edward and Rachel instilled Christian values in their children but also was an important aspect in the children's spiritual growth. No question during devotional time was too insignificant or unimportant. They took whatever time was required to answer fully all of the children's questions about the devotional topic or scripture. As the children got older, Edward and Rachel guided them in their acceptance of Christ and Edward had the meaningful and happy privilege of baptizing each of them at their home church, Eastern Antioch Baptist Church in Ogbomosho.

Susan and Stinson with new sister, Edna Rachel, 1953

Rachel with her children, 1954

Growing up on the compound

The children were fortunate to live on a compound with a large group of other children. However, their lives and activities were far different from their counterparts in the states. They participated in play outside that included climbing trees, soccer games with missionary kids and Nigerian children, and riding bicycles free of the worry of traffic. It was a carefree, idyllic life. Family board games, reading, hobbies, listening to the short wave radio and other activities that generally resulted in a close-knit family unit took the place of television and some of the social activities and pressures faced by children growing up in America. Because television was not available, the children were unaware of what they missed.

Rachel took the children with her on daily outings into town to the post office where letters from family in the states generated a great deal of excitement. These forays into downtown Ogbomosho often included shopping at the local open-air markets and weekly excursions to buy freshly butchered beef. Refrigeration was unavailable at the meat market which necessitated being present when cows were slaughtered. The beef that was purchased was taken home immediately and refrigerated.

Especially important to Edward and Rachel was their life-long love affair with music. Neither of them had learned to play a musical instrument when growing up during the hard times of the Depression, making them determined to encourage their children to do so. In fact, it was not so much a matter of whether or not to choose to do so, but rather discussions centered on which musical instruments were most desirable to learn to play. Susan and Edna Rachel quickly settled on learning to play the piano while Stinson eventually chose the flute and began taking lessons in the states when on furlough in 1959-1960. Edward and Rachel felt strongly that the lessons and instruments be available to the children although they could not easily afford to do so. All three of the children took lessons for many years; each becoming accomplished musicians to the delight of their parents.

Furlough 1955-1956

The second furlough began with rounds of visits with each of Edward and Rachel's siblings. For the first time, the children were old enough to witness the uncommon close relationship their parents had with their own siblings and cousins. It was unique and an obviously loving relationship with each. Each of their siblings insisted the family spend a few days at their respective homes. They had a deep desire for their children to know their newly acquainted cousins and to develop close relationships with their aunts and uncles. For the children, time with their relatives was an adventure and an exciting time. Their cousins acquainted them with American life—watermelon, bubble gum, Cokes in a bottle, comic books—many items taken for granted in America but not available in Nigeria and completely unfamiliar to the Humphrey children.

The year of furlough was again spent in Louisville, which allowed Edward to continue working on his doctorate. Once again, the family lived in the missionary apartments on the seminary grounds. Edward took the required preliminary written examinations and worked on his doctoral dissertation. Stinson attended public school enrolling in the first grade, which required a rather major adjustment from the sheltered environment to which he was accustomed in Nigeria.

Furlough completed, the Humphrey family returned to Nigeria via Great Britain. The first leg of the journey was aboard a passenger ship from New York to Southampton, England. On this voyage, they sailed aboard the *R.M.S. Caronia* of the Cunard Steamship Company, arriving in Southampton on August 24, 1956. Passenger ships were the favored mode of travel for missionaries in those days for a variety of reasons. Propeller-driven planes were slow, required numerous stops for refueling and flights were often turbulent. Smoking was prevalent throughout the airplane on all flights. The combination of turbulence and smoking resulted in unpleasant flights, often contributing to extended bouts of airsickness. On board large passenger ships, the family could relax together, play games and enjoy the open sea before getting back to their busy lives on the mission field. However, the final leg of the journey in the summer of 1956 was aboard one of the dreaded propeller-driven planes, across Europe, the Mediterranean, droning on across the Sahara Dessert and eventually over the lush, green tropical landscape of West Africa.

The third tour and a new home

A new home built at a new location on the compound was ready for the Humphreys when they returned from furlough. The old, large mud-constructed house no longer existed and plans were underway for construction of a smaller new home on that site for another member of the seminary faculty. The new home into which the Humphreys moved in late summer of 1956 was the home in which they resided for the remainder of the years spent in Nigeria. It was in an ideal location, not far from the new seminary buildings and adjacent to the only tennis courts on the compound where once a week, various missionaries gathered as their individual schedules allowed, for a time of socialization and tennis. The Humphrey family enjoyed their proximity to this weekly hub of social activity.

This home was the home the children would remember in later life as their primary childhood home. Constructed with cement block, it had louvered, screened-in windows, two complete bathrooms, a full kitchen, three bedrooms, a large garage with work area for Edward and a large, enclosed front porch. The home was in many respects similar to ranch style homes popular in the United States. Housing for the Humphreys had greatly improved over the original abandoned army barracks in Ede. A large tree with wide, open branches became home to a tree house built for the children by their father. Perhaps the only thing missing from the children's viewpoint was a puppy. Edward and Rachel felt strongly about not allowing them to have one because of the number of dogs with rabies.

Humphrey home, 1956-1965

Facing difficult decisions

While Edward and Rachel continued to have similar responsibilities and duties as on the previous tour, a new and more favorable prospect for school opened up for the children. Because of the large number of children within the expanding Baptist mission, a boarding school was built in the town of Oshogbo (oh-showg-bo), some thirty-five miles from Ogbomosho and only a few miles from Ede. Missionaries with teaching experience were assigned as faculty and houseparents. This represented an opportunity for the children to attend a much larger school in terms of number of students and class size. It also presented the opportunity for increased socialization and activities such as music, choir, and sports that would later enable them to better integrate into the American school system when on furlough and when the time came that their education could no longer continue in Nigeria. However, as a boarding school, it required missionary families to endure the sacrifice of sending young children away from home to attend school.

Newton Memorial School opened in Oshogbo for the school year beginning in the fall of 1956. Missionary children from all parts of Nigeria enrolled as well as some from other countries in West Africa, such as Liberia and Ghana. In 1964, Arvilla (Arvie) Oody, a student from Liberia enrolled. She and Stinson became childhood sweethearts and many years later married. A limited number of American children of parents not associated with the Baptist mission also attended. For missionaries stationed on outlying compounds, the school was a very special opportunity, for it allowed those children interaction with their peers that they would otherwise not have had. However, the distance from their parents often meant family separation for most of each semester. The Humphreys felt fortunate to be close enough to drive to Oshogbo for a Sunday afternoon visit when schedules permitted but it remained a difficult choice for any parent to send a nine or ten year old child to a boarding school in a third world country. For most parents, the many advantages of Newton School far outweighed the alternative and were felt to be in the best interest of the children. Stinson was enrolled at Newton in the fourth grade at age nine. Susan and Edna Rachel did not begin at Newton until the fifth grade after a decision was made to delay admission until children were older.

Approximately every six weeks, all children spent a long weekend away from school. For those whose homes were nearby, they went home for a time of family reunion. For those children whose parents lived too far away, they accompanied friends to their homes for the weekend. The Humphreys always opened their home for that purpose feeling it was important that every child at the school be able to take a break from the necessary discipline of a boarding school and spend a weekend in the loving embrace of family life. Edward and Rachel attempted to treat each of these children as their own on those occasions.

An even more difficult decision and time was yet to come when the children would be required to leave Nigeria to complete the final two years of high school in the United States followed by college. The topic was one Edward and Rachel avoided discussing unnecessarily for it was painful to think of the time when the family would endure extended periods of separation. For some missionaries, it was simply too difficult a choice to make, leading to early resignation from service on the mission field. Resolved in their commitment to missions, the Humphreys never considered resignation. In the end, the choice would be made for them.

Doctoral dissertation

Edward very much reveled in his role as professor at the seminary. It was exactly the type of service and work to which he felt called. He also felt it necessary to complete his doctoral degree to carry out this assignment and to fulfill his duty to the institution and to his students. He had already completed the preliminary work for the degree on their first furlough.

Preparation for his classes was of paramount importance to Edward after which he spent every moment available working on the dissertation for his doctorate during the third tour. His dedication and diligence to it were steadfast and completed with the help of his soul mate, Rachel. Almost every night after a time of family devotionals, he returned to his office to do the necessary research and to write his dissertation. Often he worked until the early morning hours. She typed what he had already written, an arduous task in the days of manual typewriters and carbon paper. The seminary in Louisville required three copies, perfectly typed without errors. It was a concerted team effort and for both a work and act of love. When the dissertation was finally completed, they sent the typed first draft to Louisville for review prior to the time they arrived for their third furlough in 1959. The diligent hard work paid off. By the time they arrived in Louisville in the fall of 1959, the dissertation entitled

"Baptist Discipline in Kentucky, 1781-1860" was already accepted and Edward lacked only the completion of his oral examination before obtaining his doctorate.

Edward with Dr. I.N. Patterson, Exec. Dir. NBM (center) and Dr. J.C. Pool, President, Nigerian Baptist Theological Seminary, 1957

Edward teaching class at NBTS

Visits with the McGees

The Humphreys felt fortunate to have Rachel's older sister, Doris and her family in Nigeria, also serving as missionaries. The McGees—John and Doris with two sons, John David and Sidney—lived in Igede. Ogbomosho and Igede were approximately one hundred miles apart or a three-hour drive in those days. The distance was far enough to prevent visits that did not involve a holiday or did not involve important mission business. The visits were a time of wonderful family celebration. These visits occurred as often as schedules allowed. The two families alternated who made the trip to the other's home on holidays, always gathering on Thanksgiving and Christmas. Visits to Igede were special. The McGees owned a horse named Rajah. Riding Rajah was always the highlight of each visit to Igede.

The visits with the McGees were occasions when both fathers took time away from their busy daily schedules to play tennis, other games and otherwise participate in all family activities. Rachel and Doris were close as sisters and enjoyed one another's company. Theirs was a special relationship, important in their lives and enjoyed by each very much. The ready availability of extended family when living in West Africa was unusual and an opportunity both families appreciated. On each of these visits, once the evening meal was completed, the families participated together in their family devotionals of Bible study and prayer. On many occasions, John then used his movie projector to show cartoons. Although the same ones were viewed over and over, they always produced a great deal of enjoyment and laughter.

On one occasion, John had mission business he needed to conduct in Ibadan, the large town about halfway between Ogbomosho and Lagos. After dropping off his family to visit in Ogbomosho, he drove on to Ibadan. Upon returning to Ogbomosho, he and his family spent the night with the Humphreys before returning to Igede. Arriving back in Ogbomosho, he first received an excited greeting from his dog, Lady, a yellow Labrador retriever. Lady ran circles around and around the yard, occasionally stopping to jump on him, offering a slobbery kiss. After several running and leaping passes by Lady, John looked at Edward and asked "Ed, what would you do if when you came back home, Rachel acted that way towards you?" Without any hesitation, Edward retorted, "I'd leave home and come back again!" The brothers-in-law were like brothers and remained so as long as they lived.

The third furlough

In July 1959, the Humphrey family packed and headed to Lagos for yet another year in Louisville where once again they lived in the missionary apartments on the campus of Southern Seminary. This furlough was the first that did not begin or end with a voyage at sea. Upon arrival at the Lagos airport, the family was astonished to see a sight they had never before witnessed. Sitting on the tarmac was a gleaming white Pan Am Boeing 707 waiting to take them in a matter of a few hours to New York. The Jet Age had arrived. The third furlough extended from the summer of 1959 through the summer of 1960. By the conclusion of that furlough, their lives had changed forever.

Edward with brother-in-law, John McGee, 1995

Unexpected Challenge

In contrast, even to faith and hope, love is what it ever shall be.
In Heaven itself, love can never be superseded; it is eternal.

Arriving in New York, the Humphreys picked up a new, two-tone green 1959 Chevrolet Impala. The car provided a means of transportation while on furlough and would be shipped to Nigeria when they returned the following year. Leaving New York, the family drove across the George Washington Bridge, heading west toward Pennsylvania. They were headed first to Pittsburgh and a reunion with two of Edward's siblings. Driving on freeways was a fascinating new experience and stark contrast to the often unpaved or washed out, single lane roads in Nigeria. In Pittsburgh, they visited with Edward's younger sister, Thetis, and his older brother, Earle, and their families. Earle's family, who lived in southern California, made special arrangements to be in Pittsburgh for the reunion. The children were thrilled to become acquainted with cousins they had never known. It was then on to North Carolina and the usual visits with family members there before returning to Louisville in time to begin the school year.

Completion of Th.D.

Edward immediately began final preparation for his upcoming oral examination, the final hurdle necessary to obtain his doctorate in theology. It had been a full decade since beginning his quest for the degree. He went about intense preparation, spending long hours at the library. When in Nigeria, he felt limited by the lack of resources and was determined to make up for lost time. Although his love was for theology, his degree was concentrated in the field of church history, the area of theological education in which the seminary in Nigeria lacked a full professor.

On November 23, 1959, the two-hour oral examination took place before the committee assigned to examine Edward. It was a cold and blustery winter afternoon. The process of working on his doctorate had been a long haul under difficult circumstances. He carried a full teaching load in addition to his other mission obligations while working on his dissertation.

The oral exam over, Edward needed time to himself. Nerves frayed, he simply did not want to face the onslaught of young children wanting his attention who could not understand his level of stress. In what seemed completely out of character to the children, Edward did not immediately return home upon completion of the examination, choosing to wait until they were ready for bed. Rachel understood the level of stress he was under leading up to the examination. She knew the high expectations and standards to which he held himself in every endeavor. Perhaps he found it difficult to be satisfied with his preparation or confident in his performance on the examination. At its conclusion, he was simply overwhelmed and spent some time alone walking, thinking and absorbing what he had been through and what he had accomplished. Edward returned home, waiting until the time when he could be alone with Rachel. It was a time to share, a time to be grateful, a time to comfort, a time to love and a time to pray.

A proud family was on hand in January 1960 when Edward received the Doctor of Theology degree (Th.D.) from Southern Baptist Theological Seminary in Louisville, Kentucky. Rachel was especially proud of him. She understood more than anyone the long hours he spent studying, working on his dissertation and preparing for exams over a ten-year period while maintaining his responsibilities as a seminary professor and missionary. Together, they rejoiced, praising God for sustaining them throughout. Rachel had arranged for the children to miss school that day so the family could celebrate together. She felt the day was cause for celebration as a family and nothing could have pleased Edward more.

Edward and family on occasion of receiving ThD January 1960

Family life in America

For the most part, the remainder of the furlough continued rather routinely. Edward accepted a teaching position at The Carver School of Missions and Social Work in Louisville for the spring semester of 1960. As the semester ended, the Board of that institution offered him a permanent position on the faculty, but Edward and Rachel's commitment was steadfastly to their original calling to missions in Africa. There was no temptation to accept the offer although an incident occurred later that spring that may well have caused them to do so save for their love of the Nigerian people and their strong commitment to their ministry in Nigeria.

For the first time, all three of the children were enrolled in public school. Edna Rachel began first grade, Susan was in fourth and Stinson, in fifth. All attended Emmet Field elementary school in Louisville and adjusted well to the public school system, excelled and became more familiar with the American way of life. Attending school in a large elementary school involved many new experiences such as carpooling, large and active playgrounds, team sports and perhaps most unusual, friends whose parents were not engaged in missions. In Nigeria, the children's playmates and schoolmates were either Nigerian or the children of missionaries. Television, albeit black and white, was available and opened up a completely new world to them. During the week, homework came first, which rarely left time for television in the evenings. The children made sure their schoolwork was finished in plenty of time to be able to watch the usual fare of Saturday morning cartoons.

The Humphrey children were encouraged to take music lessons although Edward and Rachel had a limited ability to afford them. The ability to play music was a talent they adamantly felt should be developed. Susan, who had already been taking piano lessons in Nigeria, continued taking them in Louisville. The piano lessons were given free of charge by a friend who knew Edward and Rachel when they were seminary students. A rented piano was used for practice. After much discussion, Stinson decided to learn to play the flute. A new flute was purchased in order to insure commitment and he began taking flute lessons at the University of Louisville (formerly the Louisville Conservatory of Music) in nearby Cherokee Park. The purchase of such an instrument as well as the cost of lessons was a sacrifice Edward and Rachel felt was worthwhile.

First attack of multiple sclerosis

On a bright spring Sunday morning in April, Rachel prepared breakfast in the kitchen before readying the children for Sunday school and church. Edward left earlier that morning to drive to a church out of town where he was scheduled to speak about mission work in Nigeria. Stinson vividly remembered the sense of urgency in his mother's voice when she called out to him. Reading in the next room, he rushed into the kitchen where he found his mother had cut her hand which was bleeding badly or so it seemed to him. He was certainly not prepared to deal with the amount of bleeding he saw. Telling him she could not pick up the knife she had been using seemed puzzling to Stinson, but then she said something he never forgot, "Something's wrong. I can't move." As an eleven-year-old boy, he struggled to get his mother seated in the adjoining room. He was frightened. He knew something was clearly wrong but also knew there was nothing he knew to do or could do to help her. Across the hall in an adjacent apartment, Tom and Kathy High, also missionaries in Nigeria were preparing to go to church. Responding quickly to Stinson's call, Tom found that indeed Rachel was unable to stand or walk. In what would remain a frighteningly vivid memory for Stinson, Tom literally picked Rachel up in his arms, seeming to run with her to his car. Kathy did her best to comfort the children as they watched their mother being driven to the hospital.

As was his custom, Edward left a note with the name, address and phone number of the church where he was to speak. A frantic telephone call to the church found him in the pastor's study just minutes away from being led into the service where he was to speak on missions. Edward tried his best to collect his thoughts but his focus was elsewhere. Haltingly, he began to speak. Knowing Rachel had been taken to the hospital on an emergency basis, he quickly realized the futility of his efforts. After delivering a brief synopsis of his prepared remarks, he politely excused himself. Driving directly to the hospital, he had time for his mind to wonder, to question and to think the unthinkable. What was wrong with Rachel? How serious was her condition? Would she survive? What was in store for their lives? It was too much to absorb.

Arriving at the hospital, Edward, to his surprise and relief, found Rachel lying in bed in her hospital room appearing to be very much her usual self. She had recovered much of the ability to move but unexplained neurological deficits remained. The many questions that had come to mind as he drove from the church to the hospital that day seemed distant for her condition did not appear to be as serious as he had feared.

Misdiagnosis

Rachel remained hospitalized for over two weeks as her doctors struggled to establish a diagnosis. Initially paralyzed on one side, she had the symptoms of a stroke, but miraculously, she seemed to recover more quickly than expected. Efforts to determine the cause of what had occurred took on a sense of urgency because of their impending return to Nigeria later that summer. The Foreign Mission Board required a diagnosis before allowing the Humphreys to continue living and serving where medical care was inadequately prepared to address a potentially serious illness.

Perhaps inevitably, the effort to diagnose Rachel's condition led to questioning her about her thoughts and feelings with regards to being a missionary. How did she feel about living in a third world country? Was she committed to being a missionary? In reality, were her symptoms a way of physically acting out an attempt to prevent their return to Nigeria? Was she happy living in a foreign land? Was she afraid to voice any opposition to her husband's commitment to missions? Some of the staff who examined and questioned her seemed to believe she was having a hysterical reaction to living a life she was not committed to living, in a place she did not want to be. Rachel found the line of questioning extremely offensive for her commitment to missions began long before she met Edward. She had been the one to inscribe within his wedding band the words "All That I Am." Those words were inscribed without any reservation whatsoever—both to Edward and to God. Her commitment had never been in doubt in Edward's mind. Jointly they were committed to one another and to their ministry. That anyone questioned her along these lines was deeply offensive to them both, although as was their way, they never expressed offense openly. They began, however, to recount the experience openly as if to dispel any doubt that might linger in anyone's mind.

Upon discharge from the hospital, the tests, the opinions of experts and the conclusions reached by Rachel's team of physicians did not provide a definitive diagnosis. The presumptive diagnosis was a small blood clot to her brain. Multiple sclerosis was never mentioned. Rachel was only thirty-six years old. Over the next few weeks, her recovery seemed complete but a decision by her medical team and the Foreign Mission Board about whether to allow them to return to Nigeria was uncertain. They began to prepare for news they could not bear to hear when word finally arrived from the Mission Board that they would indeed be able to return to Nigeria. Joyfully, they readied to leave Louisville for a fourth tour of mission service in Nigeria. Neither they nor her doctors were aware that she had suffered her first attack of multiple sclerosis.

The fourth tour

The family returned to Nigeria with the stipulation that Rachel required anti-coagulant therapy for the foreseeable future. She was placed on the anti-coagulant medication, Coumadin, which required that a regular blood test be performed to check the clotting time of her blood. A prothrombin-time test, the blood test used to help regulate her Coumadin dosage, was only available at the University of Ibadan medical center sixty-five miles from Ogbomosho. Throughout their remaining years in Nigeria, they were required to make regular trips to Ibadan for the test.

On returning to Nigeria, Edward and Rachel resumed the work and schedules they had left the year before. It appeared she had been fortunate to recover completely from a light stroke. Coumadin seemed to be only a precautionary form of treatment to prevent another one from occurring. Life returned to normal except for the inconvenience of regular trips to Ibadan. Stinson and Susan resumed school at Newton Memorial School in Oshogbo and Edward resumed his responsibilities as a professor at the seminary. In addition to teaching Edna Rachel and the other missionary children in Ogbomosho who were too young to attend Newton, Rachel became more involved with her teaching in the women's division of the seminary while continuing her bookkeeping duties at the leprosy center. From every vantage point, it seemed they had escaped what could have ended their mission career prematurely. Edward and Rachel found joy in their work and the children were happy at boarding school. The children were growing up feeling the love of a close-knit family unit. It was a happy time and all seemed well as they completed the fourth tour in the summer of 1963.

and he was rather matter-of-fact in telling them that their mother had been in the hospital in Ibadan where she underwent tests for rapidly spreading numbness from the waist down. The family needed to leave immediately to get her back to the states for medical treatment and, therefore, the girls needed to pack everything as quickly as possible. Their father told them he would give them the details on the way home to Ogbomosho. However, on the way home they could tell his mind was racing and absorbed by his own flooding thoughts. They left Newton without telling their friends good-bye. Would they return in a few weeks? What was wrong with their mother? Was she going to die? It felt as if they were living in the midst of a nightmare. Time seemed to stand still, while, at the same time, it seemed to be rushing by. They were in hurried motion doing as their father told them, but feeling as if they were in a daze, unable to absorb the extent of what seemed to be destroying their idyllic lives.

Once in the car, Edward spoke calmly, telling them their mother was waiting at the home of one of the missionaries in Ibadan and that they would be leaving for the states the next day. He was not particularly talkative, only briefly filling them in on the barest of details he felt they needed to know. He was in a mad dash to return to Ogbomosho to pack what he could of the family belongings and determined to let nothing interfere with getting to Lagos in time to be on the flight to New York the next morning. There were dozens of decisions to make, more things to remember, even more people to notify, and travel plans to check on—a mindboggling assortment of details that seemed to require simultaneous mental processing. More importantly, from his viewpoint, his darling was waiting in Ibadan with a potential life-threatening illness.

Leaving home

Once in Ogbomosho, Edward told his daughters to each pack one suitcase. When queried as to what they could take, he responded that they would have to make those decisions. His mind was in overload. They each packed not knowing when they would return. Susan was old enough to realize that she was likely leaving forever the place she had always called home. Edna Rachel felt she would be returning as soon as her mother received the necessary medical treatment. She could not imagine they would not return. Her birthday, September 19, was just around the corner and she noticed a small new green appliance container in her parents' bedroom. Feeling it was perhaps for her, she repeatedly asked her father what it was until in exasperation, he handed it to her and said, "Here, Happy Birthday!" His response was completely out of character. It was indeed her birthday present—an electric hair dryer. Its voltage would not allow her to use it in the states, so she left it, assuming she would enjoy it when she returned.

Edward had a myriad of things to do and decisions to make in a very short time. He also needed to pack his and Rachel's clothes, important papers, family heirlooms, pictures, a seemingly unending list of their possessions, things irreplaceable, items accumulated over a lifetime. He somehow collected his thoughts to write out instructions for the McGees who would be the ones to eventually deal with all they left behind. There was simply too much to do in the time he had left to do it. Nevertheless, news of their abrupt departure was spreading fast. A steady stream of students, their household employees, missionaries, and friends began coming by to express love and concern and to wish them well. Nigerians are a loving people and everyone wanted to help. Everyone wanted to tell them good-bye, everyone wanted assurance that all would be well and everyone looked forward to their return. Edward received every one of them graciously but the constant interruption was beginning to take its toll. He still needed to drive to Ibadan, pick up Rachel, and then go on to Lagos to catch the long flight to New York and on to North Carolina where she was expected at the Bowman Gray School of Medicine. Dr. Smith had alerted colleagues there to expect her along with his preliminary findings. Although determined not to allow them to miss the flight to New York the next day, time was running out and so was his ability to keep his mind on all the details.

Ultimately, Edward, Susan and Edna Rachel simply walked out of the house, closed the door and left everything they had not packed. The mahogany furniture he had made over the years, appliances, food on shelves, in the refrigerator and their large stand-alone freezer chest were left. They left clothes hanging on the clothesline outside. They walked out on their lives or so it seemed. For Edward, leaving was more than difficult for he had often said, "If I had a dozen lives, I would give them all to Africa." Knowing he might never return, he felt he was closing the door on the life they loved, the life to which they felt called, but something more important was now on his mind. The love of his life, his darling and the one with whom he shared his call to Africa had a serious illness and one that might well be life threatening. That thought consumed him for his call to Africa was intertwined as one with hers.

On to Lagos

As the family pulled away, it was hard to look back. Ogbomosho was home. It was the home of Susan and Edna Rachel's childhood. The sixty-five mile drive to Ibadan was quiet. Their faces pressed against the car window, they tried to memorize every detail—the people, the children waving and calling out to them as they always did, the smells, the sounds of drums beating. As they drove, one wrenching thought formed in Susan's mind that obliterated all others: "This is my home and I'm never going to see it again!" Even in the event that her mother received successful treatment, she was convinced that she would not likely be able to return.

Arriving in Ibadan in early evening, the girls were relieved to see that their mother was calm and appeared to be relatively normal except that she had difficulty walking. There was little time to visit. They were quickly on their way to Lagos. Exhausted, physically and emotionally, they arrived at the Baptist hostel in Lagos late at night. After very few hours of sleep, they were on a Pan Am jet bound for New York.

Leaving Nigeria

Once on the plane, Susan and Edna Rachel sat across the aisle from their parents but Susan watched them closely searching for clues about reactions to what was occurring in their lives. Her parents did not seem to notice for they were absorbed in serious, thoughtful conversation. Instinctively, the girls knew it was not a time to interfere or ask probing questions. They simply wanted to be good kids and refrain from adding to an already stressful situation.

Edward and Rachel were struggling with uncertainty on several fronts. Their first concern was her health but they also could not know if they had just left Nigeria forever. Would they be able to return to their adopted homeland and the people they had grown to love so deeply? Would they be able to return to the ministry to which God had called them? If they could not, what would they do? How would they financially support a family without employment? They both had longed to go to Africa as missionaries from an early age and had struggled to obtain the necessary education to get there. The ministry about which they were so passionate seemed to be slipping away. Rachel, above all the emotions she felt, was devastated. Her illness seemed to be tearing Edward away from his life's work. As she struggled with her thoughts, barely able to contain herself emotionally, Edward told her, "Whatever happens to you happens to me. We are in this together." He repeated those words many times in the days and weeks that followed. In the years that lay ahead, they were repeated numerous times in both words and actions.

After spending the night in New York, they flew on to Winston-Salem, North Carolina the next morning. There, Rachel was immediately taken to the hospital at Bowman Gray School of Medicine for registration and preliminary evaluation. Thinking back on the time, Susan said, "I don't know how Daddy did it...moving us from one world to another with a wife who suddenly couldn't walk, walking away from his life's work, virtually no sleep for two or three days. And yet the trip was bookended with the loving embrace, care and constant prayers of those in Nigeria who saw us off, and the Christian friends who received us in North Carolina, took us in, fed us, put us to sleep in beds with soft sheets, and set up appointments with the best doctors available at Bowman Gray Medical Center. By the grace and mercy of God, the trip went very smoothly."

Uncertainty

Arriving on a Monday in Winston-Salem, Rachel was hospitalized on Tuesday for thorough medical evaluation, diagnosis, and hopefully, successful treatment. It was quickly determined there was not a spinal tumor, but extensive evaluation, testing and consultations with a parade of specialists failed to establish a diagnosis. The true nature of her illness and a diagnosis was not to come for many more months.

Meanwhile, the girls needed to be enrolled in school for the school year was already well under way. Stinson was in Louisville at the boarding home, and the McGees who were on furlough at the time were also living in Louisville. Eventually, the McGees would be the ones to take on the responsibility for the Humphreys' belongings when they returned to Nigeria, but first they accepted Susan and Edna Rachel into their home and took on the responsibility of enrolling them in school. By Wednesday, the girls were in Louisville, enrolled in school on Thursday and in class on Friday! It was a tough week. They went from an average class size of five children and a student body of sixty-five to classes of thirty-five and a student body of fifteen hundred!

Events were happening far too fast for two young girls who had lived a sheltered, almost cloistered, life in Nigeria. Adjustment to life in America was difficult enough, but unfathomable just a week before. Without their parents and the unknown state of their mother's health, adjustment was all the more difficult. Their Aunt Doris and Uncle John did all they could to provide a loving home, but nothing could soothe the trauma of being jerked from the serene atmosphere of an idyllic boarding school in Nigeria and seemingly almost overnight dropped into the middle of a vibrant, throbbing American high school and junior high school. After a traumatic, difficult week in school, Edna Rachel celebrated her birthday with her siblings in Louisville. The birthday present from her parents remained back in Nigeria, but she got what she most desperately wanted, a telephone conversation with her parents and the calm soothing sound of their voices.

More than a month passed before the family was together again. Edward and Rachel came to Louisville immediately after she was discharged from Bowman Gray. They were grateful to know there was not a spinal tumor and she had regained much of her ability to walk but she had not been given a diagnosis. The immediate crisis had passed. The entire family was back together and for them, that was most important. The verses of scripture read on their wedding night once again sustained them.

Who shall separate us from the love of Christ?
Shall tribulation, or distress, or persecution, or famine, or nakedness, or peril, or sword?
As it is written, for thy sake we are killed all the day long; we are accounted as sheep for slaughter.
Nay, in all these things we are more than conquerors through him that loved us.
For I am persuaded, that neither death, nor life, nor angels, nor principalities, nor powers, nor things present, nor things to come, nor height, nor depth, nor any other creature, shall be able to separate us from the love of God, which is in Christ Jesus our Lord.

Romans 8: 35-39

Year of Transition

Godly love, like faith, is an inexhaustible theme;
and, like faith, it encompasses the whole of life.

Tears of joy flowed freely the day Edward and Rachel arrived in Louisville, having spent almost a month at Bowman Gray Medical Center. There was much to catch up on, but most importantly, the family was together again. Everyone had experienced a month of high anxiety, stress, and adjustment of enormous proportion. On this day, all of those emotions became secondary if only for a brief time.

Life goes on

Edward and Rachel remained under the employ of the Foreign Mission Board while awaiting a diagnosis that would determine whether they could return to Nigeria. Their efforts were primarily given to the establishment of a normal family life and to connecting with physicians in Louisville who could continue working toward a diagnosis for Rachel. The first order of business was to find a place for the family to live. The missionary apartments on the campus of Southern Seminary were offered without cost to furloughing missionaries but they were occupied. A missionary salary did not factor in the cost of housing, which, on the mission field, was also provided without cost. On furlough, housing for missionaries was usually provided at little cost or nothing at all because of its association with a church or some other Baptist institution. They looked for an apartment they could afford to rent that was within walking distance of the seminary and Edna Rachel's school and in an area that was not far from the boarding home for children of missionaries. Stinson and Susan needed daily transportation to Atherton High School and the boarding home offered a carpool. The area that fit their criteria was fairly well defined and offered limited possibilities. Relying on faith, they very quickly located an apartment a few blocks from the church they planned to attend, Crescent Hill Baptist Church, and in close proximity to the carpool for Stinson and Susan. It was a one-room, large studio apartment with two double beds, a pullout sofa, small kitchen and one bath. Partially underground, it was entered by walking down two steps. Small, dark and a bit dank, it nevertheless provided a home for a family overjoyed to be together.

A used Chevrolet purchased from an elderly woman who had only used it to drive to church and otherwise kept it in her garage provided transportation for the family and a mode of transportation for Edward to travel to churches in and around Louisville for the inevitable speaking engagements on Sundays. From their viewpoint, Edward and Rachel felt their needs had been met in all respects.

A semblance of normal

Within a few months, an apartment became available at the missionary apartments on the seminary campus which allowed the family to live where they had lived on four prior furloughs. They lived in that apartment for the remainder of the school year and into the following summer. Life seemed to be slowly returning to some semblance of normal. Under the circumstances, the children adjusted remarkably well to living in the states. Even the concern they felt for the health of their mother did not prevent them from becoming involved in many activities at both school and church. Considering they had taken correspondence courses in a small boarding school in West Africa, they did remarkably well in all their classes. Clearly, the love and nurturing support their parents provided served as a foundation at home upon which they built success at school. In addition, living in the missionary apartments was a settling factor the children enjoyed. Accustomed to living there on previous furloughs, their assumption was that their parents would be returning to Nigeria once a diagnosis was established and appropriate treatment rendered.

Elusive diagnosis

Holding out hope that they would be able to return to Nigeria, Edward and Rachel set about the task of seeking medical guidance that would lead to a diagnosis for what had become a mystifying illness. Consultations with numerous specialists and medical tests of all variety had so far failed to yield one, yet her symptoms persisted. Her peculiar set of neurological symptoms had thus far thwarted some of the best minds in medicine.

She remained ambulatory but she would never walk normally again. The persistent numbness, which waxed and waned, was now accompanied by tingling sensations and muscle spasms. Although she was under some of the best medical care available, the days grew darker for more and more, it looked as if they would never be allowed to return to Nigeria.

Edward spent his time accompanying Rachel to the myriad of medical appointments and, as was his way, spent countless hours researching the medical literature, determined to understand as much as he possibly could about her set of symptoms while searching for clues to her underlying illness. He purchased multiple volumes of major texts in internal medicine and neurology feeling it was important to learn what he could about her medical findings as well as wanting to better understand what the physicians were telling them. In every regard, he was a scholar and as usual prepared himself to be as well informed as he possibly could be. Better than anyone, he knew what she had been through over the past few months and diligently set about the task of learning what he could with the hope that he might be able to shed even the slightest glimmer of light on the mystery. Yet, more than a year passed without a diagnosis and the Mission Board was beginning to raise questions about the viability of there ever being a chance for them to return to Nigeria. Time was running out.

The door to foreign missions begins to close

As the summer of 1966 approached, it was becoming increasingly clear that the Humphreys would soon have no choice but to resign from the mission field and their appointment as missionaries to Nigeria. Their status with the Mission Board was officially a leave of absence, but other factors contributed to a fast approaching date when they felt they must resign. The seminary in Nigeria needed to find a permanent replacement for Edward on the faculty. The Mission in Nigeria needed their unoccupied home for other missionaries. As was their nature, they, too, were concerned about those factors. While never their desire to resign prematurely from the mission field, they wanted to be completely open, forthright and fair with the Mission Board and the Mission in Nigeria. The longer they went without a diagnosis, what seemed to be an inevitable resignation drew ever closer. Ultimately, it was the responsibility of the Foreign Mission Board and their medical personnel to make the decision from a medical viewpoint whether they were, in fact, able to return to Nigeria.

Trusting God

Although a decision was a few months away, Edward began feeling concerned about employment should they not be able to continue their work in Nigeria. He undertook numerous speaking engagements at various churches in and around Louisville in the interim and began to think and talk about returning to the ministry as pastor of a church. Simultaneously, he began to explore the possibility of finding a teaching position in theological education. Toward that end, he wrote letters and began a process of networking as best he could. As usual, he spent a great deal of time reading and studying in the seminary's library. This time he not only studied the medical texts, but also spent considerable time in the process of catching up in all fields of theological education. He wanted to be prepared should any teaching position become available at a seminary anywhere in the United States.

It was a stressful time. Anxiety about Rachel's health was high. Responsibility for a young family weighed heavily. Stinson and Susan were fast approaching the time they wanted to continue their education at the college level. Edward and Rachel were ill prepared for the financial aspects of that eventuality. Were they able to remain officially employed by the Foreign Mission Board, the children would receive substantial college scholarships but early retirement or resignation meant those scholarships would be lost. In spite of their concerns, they never deviated from their faith or from their trust in God. Their faith and trust was an integral part of their lives and always had been. It always would be. Although it was clear to the children that it was an anxious time, it was also clear their parents never doubted for a moment that God had a plan for their lives and would provide for their needs. Growing up in that environment of trust and faith, attending college was a chance the children never doubted they would have. Meanwhile, they concentrated on achieving high grades in school, engaged in extracurricular school activities and enjoyed a robust social life.

Breakthrough

As the summer of 1966 progressed, Edward and Rachel knew there was little chance of ever returning to Nigeria. Officially, they remained on a leave of absence from the Foreign Mission Board. That status could not continue indefinitely yet her medical team was at a loss to give her a firm diagnosis. Certain she had some type of neurological disorder;

they were unable to pinpoint it further. Therefore, Edward's efforts to identify potential areas of permanent employment increased in intensity. The stress under which they lived was beyond comprehension unless viewed through their unyielding trust and faith in God.

Telephone calls into a home with three teenagers during evening hours rarely came for either Edward or Rachel. Thus, no one expected the call from Dr. Harold Graves, President of Golden Gate Baptist Theological Seminary in Mill Valley, California. Calling to speak to Edward, he inquired about the possibility of Edward coming to California for one semester to teach courses in theology at Golden Gate Seminary. Everyone was excited, but for different reasons. Edward and Rachel felt some measure of relief. At the very least, this bought some limited time, perhaps more, to secure more permanent employment. The children viewed this turn of events from a much different perspective. Never in their wildest imagination had they thought of living in California. However, they continued to think in terms of their parents eventually returning to Nigeria. Susan and Edna Rachel faced, yet again, an almost unimaginable change in their lives. On the other hand, Stinson could hardly believe what he heard, for his girlfriend from Newton School, whose parents were missionaries in Liberia were on furlough—in California! Following a formal interview and visit with Edward, Dr. Graves asked him to come to Golden Gate as visiting professor of philosophy and theology. It was to be for only one semester but everyone was thrilled. Edward quickly began preparing to spend a semester away from the family as well as studying for the courses he would be teaching.

In late August, Edward flew to California to begin teaching at Golden Gate Seminary. When he left Louisville, Edward and Rachel remained uncertain as to what the future held. Expecting him to return in December, they decided they did not want the children to face another uprooting move of such short duration. They made the decision that Rachel would stay with the children in Louisville to provide some stability in their lives. Changing schools for one semester was simply too disruptive. Shortly after Edward arrived in California, Dr. Graves asked him to extend the teaching position to a full year, suggesting that he might bring his family to be with him in California. Officially, they remained on a leave of absence from the mission field, but their belief in God's immutable plan for their lives remained steadfast. This new opportunity would allow them to continue their calling to a life in His service and once again, they felt they were upon the "high road."

New Ministry

In the freedom of His own love, God makes us free:
free to hear His call, to receive His word, to dwell in His presence, and
to seek His glory

Final word had not yet come from the Foreign Mission Board regarding the possibility of returning to Nigeria by the time the entire family was planning their move to California. Their ministry in Nigeria was one Edward and Rachel felt they had not completed. Although both were eager to return, they knew the decision was not theirs to make. God's plan for their lives would play out in due course. For now, they would be patient, trust in Him and live filled with hope for whatever the future held.

Moving west

The family was thrilled when Edward called to tell them the news. Plans developed quickly for the move to California and within a few days, the family was on a flight to San Francisco and to another family reunion. Once there, the children enrolled in school. Although, it was the fourth school in which they had enrolled in as many years, the family was grateful to be together again. The prior year had been a difficult year and they were certain they soon faced the decision of whether or not they would return to Nigeria.

There was no faculty housing per se at Golden Gate nor were there missionary apartments. The seminary provided housing for the Humphreys in a student apartment on Lockett Lane. It was a two-bedroom apartment with one bath, somewhat smaller than the missionary apartments in Louisville and within walking distance of Edward's office and classrooms. They purchased a new car and sold the used car left in Louisville. A car and the ability to drive was important to Rachel as she adjusted to a new community, new friends, a new church and an overwhelming desire to provide her children with some semblance of a normal life. Transportation allowed the children to more quickly integrate into new schools and socialize with new friends. In private conversations, she continued to feel a sense of guilt, feeling she was the one who deprived Edward of carrying on his ministry in Nigeria. Repeatedly, he reiterated, "Whatever happens to you happens to me. We are in this together." In an effort to allay Rachel's sense of guilt, he began to speak in terms of, "This happened to both of us. It's our problem."

Diagnosis established

On moving to California, physicians there assumed responsibility for Rachel's care and the establishment of a definitive diagnosis. She was admitted to the University of California, San Francisco Medical Center for further testing within a few weeks of moving. This hospitalization ultimately resulted in the diagnosis of multiple sclerosis, an autoimmune disease of the central nervous system. It had been over a year since they left the mission field and they could finally feel some sense of relief in knowing a diagnosis. What had been merely a set of symptoms finally had a name. However, establishment of a diagnosis made them acutely aware that a decision was imminent regarding the possibility of returning to Nigeria. They prepared for news they did not want to receive.

Within a few weeks, Edward and Rachel's fears were realized. As they suspected, the diagnosis of multiple sclerosis resulted in the Board's decision not to allow them to return to Nigeria. The most heartfelt emotions, feelings and conversations they had with one another at the time remained private. They were clearly disappointed, perhaps even devastated but they accepted the decision with grace and knew it was the correct one. Believing in His plan for their lives, they prayerfully turned to God for new direction. The manner in which they lived the remainder of their lives spoke volumes regarding their faith.

Refocusing

Edward and Rachel quickly set about the task of refocusing their lives. Her health would always be of primary concern, but they were determined to live with any limitations imposed by multiple sclerosis. Already, they knew there were many yet to come their way but they were resolved to prevent the disease from interfering with their ministry.

The first order of business was to retrieve what remained of their personal belongings in Nigeria. The McGees, on returning to Nigeria in the summer of 1966, graciously undertook the arduous task of sorting through what had been hurriedly left behind in Ogbomosho. They were the ones who had the difficult task of making decisions regarding the Humphreys' personal possessions. They would decide what was to be shipped or sold. Without a complete inventory of what was left, Edward and Rachel gave John and Doris only general instructions in order to make the task as simple as possible. Included in the items shipped were his treasured books, collected over a lifetime. He had a small library primarily of books associated with his teaching but some that once belonged to his father, Stinson. These had great sentimental value. The furniture he had built over their years in Nigeria was, by necessity, sold, for it was far too expensive to ship. It was an experience they were grateful they did not face themselves.

Once the shipment was readied, it followed a long and circuitous route from Nigeria to California. Many weeks passed without any sight or word on the whereabouts of their belongings. Eventually, some of the crates that were shipped found their way to Canada and into the hands of a family who painstakingly found a way to contact the Humphreys and forward the crates on to California. Others, including many of their personal valuables were either stolen or forever lost. Never ones to be materialistic, Edward and Rachel found joy in what they did ultimately receive, most importantly, his books.

New roots established

Many years after moving to California, Edward, in responding to a question regarding the difficulty of the transition from Nigeria said, "Yes, when we first came to Golden Gate, I thought I would never feel at home...now, of course I do." Settling into their new lives with determination and a renewed sense of mission, they joined a new church, Tiburon Baptist Church and through the seminary and church made many new friends. The children, with new friends, were adjusting well to new schools. The family quickly developed an extended family, much like the mission family in Nigeria, only now it consisted of their seminary family and church family. Each provided stability and a sense of belonging.

Rachel managed responsibilities at home but soon, the physical limitations brought on by multiple sclerosis became even more apparent, slowly and inexorably progressing over the ensuing years. Laundry facilities, in a building up the hill from their apartment on Lockett Lane, required that she climb several sets of stairs, which she found increasingly difficult. Initially, she was able to manage with the aid of the rail alongside the steps but soon this became too difficult and she began to drive to a Laundromat so that she could remain on level ground. Difficulty walking was among the first of many functional physical disabilities she encountered throughout many years of ever-increasing dysfunction. Spreading numbness resulted in frequent burns that, for a short time, went unnoticed. She resolved to do her best to stave off the inevitability of an increasing number of physical disabilities and the accompanying emotional distress they caused. Facing the realities of her disease, she knew that the day would come when she could no longer perform routine tasks and would slowly lose the ability to be physically active, something she was unaccustomed to in the life she had led in Nigeria.

Rachel remained deeply involved with the lives of her children. As they became more and more involved in school and church activities, she continued to love and support them in every endeavor. Stinson and Susan enrolled at Tamalpais High School in Mill Valley as a senior and junior. Edna Rachel was in eighth grade at Edna Maguire Junior High School. Considering the change, chaos and turmoil they had experienced over the past two years, all three adjusted well and excelled in their educational endeavors. Stinson, who only attended one year of high school in California, decided to return to the southeastern part of the country for college, attending Carson Newman College, a small liberal arts school in Tennessee, in order to be with his girlfriend, Arvie. Susan felt the need for some stability in her life and looked toward staying near home for college, attending the University of California at Berkeley. Edna Rachel was not yet at the point of considering college but would eventually attend California State University Sacramento. Following the example set by their parents, each of the children pursued post-graduate education. After graduating from college, Stinson obtained degrees in dentistry and medicine while Susan and Edna Rachel each obtained advanced degrees in nursing.

Rachel developed close friendships with other faculty wives. She wanted to be useful and helpful and missed the busy work of her active life in Nigeria. As she always had done since the onset of symptoms, she looked to how she could find useful projects within the confines of her limitations. She began by acting as a conduit for other faculty wives, telephoning them to remind them of meetings and to arrange carpools. In an attempt to maintain use of her hands, she began doing needle art, usually crewel, as well as embroidery. Her art hung in many of her friends' homes. As the years passed, she made special mementos for family members, especially for each of her grandchildren. With each piece, she attempted to make something that was special and meaningful for the person receiving her gift of love.

Edward became thoroughly engaged in his teaching responsibilities, finding satisfaction and fulfillment in the courses he taught. Now that he knew her diagnosis, he began an intense study of multiple sclerosis in the medical literature. He was determined to stay abreast of new treatment modalities but moreover was preparing himself for what was to come as her disease progressed. As a couple, they were aware of the hardships they faced and did their best to prepare themselves. Outwardly, they remained positive, upbeat and optimistic. Often, Rachel spoke of a time when there would be a cure for her disease. Never did she complain or give voice to disillusionment or anger. Her trust and faith in God gave her amazing adaptability as well as the strength and ability to take one day at a time. Visitors asking how she was feeling received the same straightforward and positive answer, "Fine, thank you." The answer remained consistent the remainder of her life.

Golden Gate becomes home

In March 1967, the Board of Trustees of Golden Gate Baptist Theological Seminary voted to elect Edward Associate Professor of Historical Theology and research librarian. Edward and Rachel felt their calling to a life in His service had new direction and rejoiced in their new ministry. They lived on Lockett Lane for two years until in 1968 new faculty housing constructed on the seminary campus became available. Their new home on Platt Court was a short walking distance down the hill from his office and classrooms. It would be their home until retirement in 1983.

As they continued on the "high road" of their ministry, they found joy and hope in the love they shared for one another and for God. Each was the true complement of the other and they experienced a blissful life as *one* in marital union. They found much happiness in their new ministry as well as their shared family life and it was abundantly clear to all around them. When writing about their journey through life, Edward described their love and life together as "a lovely symphony." They never openly expressed any bitterness regarding the inability to return to Nigeria although it was without doubt painful. Rachel said, "When the Lord closed one door, He opened another. We follow His will day by day." Fully accepting of God's plan for their lives, they continued their journey together fulfilled by their faith, sustained by their trust in God, never losing hope and always deeply in love.

Their devoted love for one another and the children provided stability, a foundation and an example the children would take with them throughout their own lives and into their own marriages. Their home was a loving home, a place that under any circumstance was a haven of love. It was a home where voices never were raised, where arguments did not occur, where anger was never uncontrolled and where support was never withheld. Edward and Rachel were well aware that the children went through many unsettling changes in their lives during these years. Resolute in their commitment to make theirs a stable, happy, and loving home, they did so by example.

A unique ministry

Edward and Rachel shared a unique ministry in California; one they did not fully comprehend for many years and one that they were unwilling to speak of publicly in terms of its far-reaching influence on others. Perhaps their humility prevented them from doing so. All who encountered them took away a sense of their complete faith and trust in God. All who knew them knew they loved one another with deep, unreserved commitment. No one who knew them, individually or as a couple, ever doubted their complete faith in God. No one doubted their love for God. No one doubted their love for one another. They lived as examples of devoted love, of unselfish love, of undying love, of love eternal. For them, their faith and love did "encompass the whole of life." They became a source of strength to all who knew them.

Throughout their life journey, they became examples to emulate. A fellow church member wrote, "Dr. and Mrs. Humphrey are both scholars; both are blessed saints. Others might wonder why God allowed such tragedy to befall two who were so faithful. They do not question. They just accept. They rest under the wings of God."

144

Edward & Rachel at Platt Court apartment, 1972

Love Conquers All

Where love controls, presence is not so much a spatial concept as it is a genuine openness for the other's needs.

Rachel's comprehension of what she faced with multiple sclerosis came from firsthand experience within her own family. Not long after her own diagnosis, she learned her niece who had been the flower girl in their wedding was also diagnosed with multiple sclerosis. A particularly aggressive form of multiple sclerosis affected her niece that resulted in death before forty years of age. Her oldest sister, Lela Mae, suffered with the disease as well. She too had gone through a long process of diagnosis, ultimately learning that she had multiple sclerosis after Rachel was diagnosed. Rachel was aware that she was unable to prevent the progressive neurological effects of her disease but was determined to keep herself in the best possible state of health. She was also aware that her disease would have a huge impact on the sweetheart of her life, Edward. It would be enormous but she was resolved to be as independent for as long as she could. Sadly, her independence did not last long.

Multiple Sclerosis

Multiple Sclerosis is an autoimmune disorder in which the patient's own body essentially attacks itself, resulting in the destruction of the myelin sheath that surrounds nerves in the central nervous system. The body itself attacks the protein in that protective coating of myelin around the nerves in the brain and spinal cord, a process called demyelination. The scarring caused by these attacks is termed sclerosis. Various symptoms result depending on where the damage occurs and which nerves are affected. Rachel's symptoms initially included numbness, tingling, burning sensations, fatigue, and then a loss of balance, muscle control and strength. As the disease progressed, she developed a myriad of additional symptoms.

Each patient with multiple sclerosis is unique. Symptoms vary from patient to patient. Both sensory and motor nerves undergo demyelination. Each patient has symptoms that are dependent on which of their nerves undergo the process of demyelination. The progression of the disease varies in each patient as well. Some patients have very mild cases in which progression of the disease is slow. Some cases lead very rapidly to confinement in a wheelchair or bed. Aggressive cases result in early death. No medical test was available that could determine, in advance, the course Rachel's illness would take.

Rachel's activities narrow

Rachel began a regimen of exercise along with physical therapy. Her loss of balance and difficulty walking prevented her leaving home for exercise and, therefore, limited the types of exercise she was able to do. She was not able to go on long walks, run, or swim. Those required her to be ambulatory. With limited choices, she decided the best form of exercise was riding a stationary bicycle, which she was diligent in doing every morning. Initially, she could ride when Edward was in class, but, as her sense of balance diminished, she had to do it before he left for class or after he returned. Initially, he took her for supervised physical therapy. Together they learned a routine of resistance exercises, stretching, and muscle strengthening using a workout regimen with light weights. Eventually, he became her physical therapist in their home. For the rest of her life, he was diligent, conscientious and very adept with her physical therapy. They rose early each morning to accomplish her physical therapy and exercises that required his assistance before he left for class. He dressed, made beds and helped her with resistance exercises. She then dressed and rode the stationary bicycle while he prepared breakfast. After he left for class, she continued with the exercises that she could do on her own without risk of falling, such as the muscle strengthening exercises. Coping with multiple sclerosis was a team effort with the goal of limiting progression of the disease or unnecessary side effects as best they could.

Soon after moving to Platt Court, Rachel made the decision she could no longer safely drive. After losing her independence, she was homebound unless Edward or some other person was available to take her out. Friends and family accompanied her shopping and to the hairdresser. Edward made a point of taking her out to lunch every Friday—something she looked forward to that very soon became the high point of her week. She also looked forward to one of her favorite pastimes, playing Scrabble. She played it well and was the expert among her friends and family. She always had the patience to play with others less skilled at the game, including children. She enjoyed the time it gave her with friends, many of whom came often and regularly.

Inevitably, her ability to walk became more and more diminished. In the relatively short period of four to five years, she progressed in steps from walking with a cane to wearing lower leg braces and then to using a walker. By 1973, she required the use of a wheelchair to get about the house as well as when away from home. Determined to maintain independence and a sense of usefulness, she continued to do as much as she could around home. She continued to prepare meals, but did so from the wheelchair, straining to reach the rear of countertops and the stovetop. Rolling herself about the house, she continued to do as much of the housekeeping as she was able. Determined to keep her independence for as long as possible, she would not allow her disease to limit unnecessarily what she was able to do. Each relinquished step in her diminishing ability to move came about only after she was thoroughly convinced it was necessary, usually because of a fall or some minor injury that frightened her.

After Rachel's first fall, Edward decided he should telephone her after each of his classes. If there were no answer, he raced down the hill, usually to find she had fallen without injury but unable to get up because of insufficient muscle strength. On one occasion, he found she had fallen, was unable to get up and clearly dazed. Subsequent evaluation determined she had suffered a minor concussion. Together, they made the decision she could no longer stay alone and someone was hired to stay with her during the hours he was in class.

Adaptation to multiple sclerosis

Edward and Rachel made many changes to help her adapt to the limitations imposed by her disease. Some she imposed herself; others were the result of his help and ingenuity. In the kitchen, knives were never left carelessly about for she might lose her balance and fall on one or accidentally lay her hand on one when reaching from the wheelchair. She was very careful when using the gas stove. Without realizing it, she could badly burn herself were a flame left ignited and unnoticed. The same was true in the shower. Getting in without testing water temperature could possibly result in severe burns. She discovered that an area of skin on the top of her shoulders still had enough feeling to discern whether water was too hot. Edward purchased a sitting stool for the shower so she would not lose her balance when bathing and, for the first time, they purchased a television with remote control. Living with multiple sclerosis would lead to many more adaptations in the future.

Edward settles into a new career

Edward missed the foreign mission field and missed the work he left in Nigeria, but at Golden Gate, he was teaching the subjects he loved most and became increasingly happy in his work there. In Nigeria, the classes he taught were primarily in church history. At Golden Gate, he was able to concentrate on the areas of Christian education he loved most—theology, specifically, systematic theology[16] and historical theology[17] as well as philosophy. He worked hard to prepare for his classes, often studying late into the night, determined to pass on to his students the understanding of God he had learned from his own close relationship with Him founded in faith. He had high expectations of his students and often lingered after class to discuss any topic to whatever length his students wished. His students appreciated his thoroughness and remembered him as highly intellectual and a well-organized, conscientious teacher. Referring often to his ministry in Nigeria, he once told his students, "King David said in the Psalms that he had 'never seen the righteous forsaken or their children begging bread'" (Psalm 37: 25) but went on to tell them that perhaps King David never saw that but he did—in Nigeria! Near the end of his life, he gave many of the books in his extensive library to former students and donated the remainder to the library at Golden Gate to be given to students who needed or wanted them.

One of those students to whom he gave many of his books was Nelson Hayashida, himself now a missionary in Africa, along with his wife, Sandra. Sandra's parents had been missionaries in Ghana, and she attended Newton School at the time Stinson and Susan were

---

[16]   A systematic study of God and Biblical teachings about God.

[17]   A study of how Christians have viewed God historically

there, remaining close friends throughout the years. After Sandra met and married Nelson, he enrolled at Golden Gate Baptist Theological Seminary where he developed a close relationship with his theology professor, Edward Humphrey. During their years at the seminary, Nelson and Sandra took a special interest in both Edward and Rachel and remained in close contact after Edward's retirement. Nelson, when asked to contribute to this volume, remembered Edward as:

"...someone who desired to emulate his God. His humility somehow must be how he viewed God to be, I suppose.

Edward Humphrey was pure cedar, as tall, rich and enduring as those in Lebanon.

For me, he was preeminently a kind and conscientious person. Not surprisingly, he utilized those character traits in his fundamental approach to philosophy and theological language. As a consequence, his affectionate affair with and care for words and the thoughts behind them led him deep and wide into the arena of intellectual affirmations of Divinity and the pitfalls of sentimentality.

I recall one lecture at Golden Gate seminary; oh, it could have been around 1975. On this occasion, Dr. Humphrey was speaking about the Holy Spirit and his natural and theological distaste for any reference to the Holy Spirit as 'sweet.' The professor reminded the class of the song, 'there's a sweet, sweet Spirit in this place, and I know that it's the Spirit of the Lord.' As a young seminarian, I disagreed with this kind and gentle man. I loved this song, and there is a side of God that is sweet. Surely! But he asked: 'What is sweet about the Holy Spirit? There is nothing sweet about him. The Holy Spirit is not something that's sugar-coated, either physically or metaphorically.' Whatever his exact words were, that was what I believe the kind and conscientious man was saying to us.

I didn't know what he was driving at, really. Why would he belabor such a point? I see now that while I saw him trying to communicate from a rational point of view, he was essentially not doing so. He was communicating from a more secure place, from his core. He was communicating powerfully from his heart as a conscientious Christian. He was declaring something like – 'don't trivialize God, don't popularize the Holy Spirit with a feel-

good hymn, don't romanticize your faith and thereby cheapen it; the Holy Spirit is more profound, and offers grace and strength in ways of mystery yet to be experienced, much less appreciated, by most of us, so don't sentimentalize the walk of discipleship.'

Now I see the lesson. Sandra reminds me that my personal admiration for Dr. Humphrey had a lot to do with the humble, intellectual servant who adjusted his entire career to care for his homebound wife Rachel. Edward and Rachel understood the hard knocks of life. The Holy Spirit, as cedar, offered grace and strength on a daily basis. Rachel was his ministry.

As a missionary in Africa, again, I've tried not to trivialize truth. The approach to my spiritual journey I owe in part to the professor. I try, in spite of the weaknesses of my sinful humanity, to sink deeper and more seriously into Jesus and the faith of that eternal relationship. I thank Uncle Edward for helping me do that.

In the beginning of this reflection, I said Edward Humphrey was a kind and conscientious person. He was so with me. He was so with his beloved wife until the day and moment she died. And he was so with the strength of his theological contemplations.

What I would give to hear a coffee table conversation between the 'process theologians' Alfred North Whitehead and Charles Hartshorne with Edward Humphrey on the topic 'God as the Unchanging and Passionless Absolute.' I am sure there would be agreement and disagreement. The kind and conscientious one would be in good company! The only triviality would be the fly on the wall, me."

Supporting one another

Edward and Rachel realized that they both required additional emotional support to be able to cope with a disease they faced and endured together. From the beginning, he said, "It is our problem." She often told people, "a cure is around the corner." Each was dependent on the other. Each had their own way of supporting the other. Each openly expressed their love for the other. Most importantly, they had implicit faith and trust in God. They were confident in His love. Edward never left home without affectionately telling her that he loved her and giving her a kiss. She was his "darling" and she knew it and heard it frequently. He was an affectionate husband and father, displaying his affection freely and openly as his own father had done. Arriving home, whether for the noon meal or in the evening, he went to each family member individually with open affection. She was always the last and he paused a little longer, a bit more affectionately and with special intensity. She was the most beautiful woman he had ever known, and he told her. Expressions of love were heartfelt and frequent. Never was there any doubt about her place in his heart and mind.

Rachel looked forward to Edward's return from class. He was her "sweetheart" and he knew it and he heard it frequently. She was an affectionate wife and mother who displayed her love and affection freely and openly. Meals were never served until he got home. When he did get home, she watched him go to each of the others and gazed intently into his eyes when he got to her. She was always in high spirits when he came home and she listened and was supportive in a way no one else could. He was the most handsome man she had known, and she told him. Expressions of love were heartfelt and frequent. Never was there doubt about his place in her heart and mind.

Edward went to great lengths to keep Rachel informed about his classes, his students and the book he was writing. She listened intently, asked probing questions, lent an understanding ear and always offered words of encouragement. She talked about her day, her conversations, the children and her own special problems. He responded in his usual caring way and with ingenuity, able with his own efforts to meet most of her needs or provide a method for her to adequately deal with them.

In the mornings before Edward left for class, they had their devotional time together. Beginning their day with Bible reading, discussion and prayer, they relied on this special time together to sustain them. They trusted God and never doubted His love. Remarkably, they both lived within the confines imposed by multiple sclerosis without any bitterness, never asking "Why?" or "Why us?" They did their best to live the form of godliness, as they understood it. Living a godly life had always been the focus of their lives together and its form was central to their thinking and manner of life.

Love and Family

Love is a way of life, and its forms are uniquely its own.

Close family bonds were a treasured, consistent part of the Humphrey's lives. The children grew up experiencing the loving embrace of those bonds from earliest memory. Over the years, Edward and Rachel made certain they were always available to their children and by example, lived their own lives as ideal examples of a godly life. The family lived in California for only a short time before the children one by one, began to leave home for college to follow their dreams. Each left with open, heartfelt parental support and unconditional love.

Extended family members were an important part of those family bonds upon which Edward and Rachel relied. They stayed in close touch with siblings and cousins through frequent letters, telephone calls and visits. Edward was proud of his double-first cousins (the children from families of parents who are siblings who marry siblings). Visits to North Carolina by Edward and Rachel were cause for large family reunions while both siblings and cousins visited them frequently, enjoying quiet and quality time.

A family affair

Multiple sclerosis afflicted only one family member yet inevitably affected the entire family. It seemed only natural for all three of the children to become involved early on with the constraints imposed by the disease. They did so out of love—a love generated by observing the many facets of love so readily apparent in the way their parents lived. Many opportunities to demonstrate their love and concern for both parents came in unexpected ways in the years that followed. The family was a one-car family living in a car-oriented California society. Financial circumstances did not allow for a second car and not long after arriving in California, Rachel was no longer driving. These limitations not only forced the children to seek alternative means of transportation but also to assume the responsibility of driving their mother to various places and for various outings when Edward was unavailable.

In Nigeria, the family was accustomed to a vibrant and energetic mother who was involved in every aspect of her family's activities. Stinson, who at thirteen years of age, took note of feminine grace and beauty watching his mother walk across the room, had to adjust to the progressive, debilitating and crippling nature of multiple sclerosis, for very soon she needed assistance with essentially all of the routine tasks of daily living. Each of the children responded and adapted in their own way to their mother's altered lifestyle and the limitations imposed by her disease.

Education—a family tradition

Edward and Rachel believed education to be an essential component of truth and the understanding of life. They had been relentless in their own pursuit of an education and had steadfastly believed life itself was a continuum of learning. They sought to learn at every opportunity and with each new experience. Growing up, their own families encouraged each of them in their educational endeavors and they instilled the importance of it in their own children. Stinson, Susan and Edna Rachel grew up with the expectation that they would one day attend college. Edward and Rachel spoke frequently of the ordeal of their own education providing their children with an example of the hard work, determination and sacrifice required. As supportive and loving parents, they were parents who engendered in their children a strong desire to please. They were parents who were never demanding, never critical, never overbearing, and always encouraging of each of their children to pursue individual goals. Delighted with success, they never admonished them to do better and never expressed disappointment or shame. To "do your best" was what they expected. Stability, support and love were what they provided. All of these qualities in Edward and Rachel served to motivate each of the children to excel in their educational pursuits.

Susan and Edna Rachel went on to complete nursing programs following their undergraduate education and continued on to become highly specialized within their respective fields—Susan as an intensive care neonatal nurse and Edna Rachel as a coronary care intensive care nurse. Both enjoyed very successful careers in their chosen field. Their parents derived a great deal of pride and satisfaction in their achievements and success.

After completing his undergraduate education, Stinson also entered the medical field, obtaining doctorates in both dentistry and medicine. He practiced medicine in San Jose, California after completion of his residency at Vanderbilt University Medical Center. Edward and Rachel helped each of their children in immeasurable ways to succeed throughout the course of each of their educations. Expressions of love, support, encouragement and pride never failed to engender the determination to do better, to please and to succeed.

When grandchildren came along, Edward and Rachel reveled anew with the school drawings, science projects, term papers and the inevitable questions that came their way. The importance of education was a strong family tradition that began with Edward's father, Stinson. Edward and Rachel were successful in passing on that tradition to succeeding generations.

A lifetime of learning

Edward was a continuous student throughout his life. When asked his plans for the evening, the predictable response was, "I'll be studying." As a lifelong student, he yearned to learn more. He always felt he could be better prepared to teach his classes. His students deserved his very best effort. He labored to choose the best words with which to get across the subject matter, his thoughts and ideas. He loved words and developed an unusual ability to express himself with eloquence whether with spoken or written words.

Edward was eligible for a year of sabbatical after seven years at Golden Gate. Rachel's illness prevented travel to a faraway place where she would not have access to her physicians who were actively treating her multiple sclerosis. Therefore, Edward looked for a nearby suitable higher center of learning that would meet his and the seminary's expectations for the sabbatical year. He enrolled at the Graduate Theological Union in Berkeley, California for the year where he enjoyed a variety of classes and work at what is a union of several member seminaries and theological institutions. He very much enjoyed not only his study there but also his interaction with a wide variety of members of interdenominational faiths.

With encouragement from Rachel, he began writing his first book; a scholarly study of the theology of Emil Brunner, one in a series of books published under the title, *Makers of the Modern Theological Mind*, edited by Dr. Bob E. Patterson of Baylor University. Over the course of researching and writing his book in the series, Rachel was always supportive and the one he chose for discussion of ideas and critique. He valued her judgment. She loved being a part of the process. They viewed the project as a joint effort, the way they viewed all endeavors. *Emil Brunner* was published in 1976 and dedicated by Edward,

> *For Rachel*
> *dear companion in*
> *life and faith*

Rachel was proud of Edward, proud of the book and never shied from touting his intellectual and writing abilities. She had been patiently and quietly supportive, encouraging him as he spent long evening hours in his study working on the book. She knew it was important to him and therefore important to her.

Family time

Rachel's disease limited the traveling they were able to undertake. Trips were taken only when considered a necessity or were ones Edward and Rachel decided was important. Traveling required great effort for both of them. Her problems with ambulation and the myriad of other symptoms made overnight visits away from home difficult and stressful. Travel of any great distance or that involved an overnight stay was usually limited to visiting immediate and extended family members. John and Doris McGee, with whom they so often visited when in Nigeria, were able to visit them in California on several occasions. The two couples had not seen one another as frequently as when in Nigeria and therefore, their visits were special times of catching up and reminiscing. Over the years, the Humphreys ventured out of state on rare occasion and only back east to visit family. In 1970, they visited family in North Carolina prior to going to Tennessee for the wedding of Stinson and Arvie. That would be Rachel's last visit with her mother. Elsie died in May 1978, just before they planned to visit her in July. After visiting with their siblings in July 1978, they went on to Nashville, Tennessee to visit Stinson and Arvie and to celebrate the birth of their first granddaughter who was born while they were visiting in North Carolina. One generation had passed as a new one had come into their lives. Their sadness at the loss of one yielded to love and hope for another. They were especially pleased to learn their new granddaughter was named Rachel.

Rachel with her mother, Elsie, 1970

Rachel with her granddaughter and namesake, Rachel, 1978

Edward and Rachel, 1978

In-state trips were more frequent. Regular visits occurred with their children and grandchildren. It was important to create memories, especially with the grandchildren. Trips to visit with Edward's brother Earle were frequent. The brothers enjoyed a close relationship and each admired the other for their accomplishments. When visiting, countless hours were spent reminiscing, telling stories, laughing and remembering the good times of days gone by. Edward and Rachel also enjoyed the short trips to the Asilomar Conference Center in Monterey for seminary faculty retreats. An escape from a near-homebound lifestyle, these trips were nevertheless tiring and difficult for both of them. Being away from home was troublesome for her with her varied disabilities and he spent much of the time concerned about her. They enjoyed the contact with fellow faculty members and their spouses as well as the outside world and change in scenery, but were always happy when it was time to return home.

Love and marriage

Each of the three Humphrey children married during the 1970's. Edward composed the ceremony and vows that each couple used for their wedding. The ceremony he composed became a part of family tradition, later used by his grandchildren at their weddings. In many ways, the ceremony he composed expressed his feelings and love for Rachel. Stinson married Arvilla (Arvie) Oody, his girlfriend from Newton School in Oshogbo, Nigeria in 1970. They were married in Loudon, Tennessee. Both Susan and Edna Rachel were married at Tiburon Baptist Church in Tiburon, California. Susan married Brian Perkins in 1976 and Edna Rachel married Sandy Miller in 1978. Edward officiated at each of his children's weddings as well as presenting his daughters at the marriage altar. With each new addition to their family, Edward and Rachel rejoiced and shared in the happiness each couple experienced. Each new spouse was viewed as another son or daughter with whom they each developed a close relationship.

The Humphreys rarely were able to entertain large groups in their home but in May 1972, Susan and Edna Rachel helped them open their home to friends and family from Golden Gate Seminary and Tiburon Baptist Church to celebrate their 25th wedding anniversary. Edward used the occasion to give Rachel a small diamond necklace and, as he had done on many previous occasions, put his thoughts and feelings to words in the form of an anniversary letter.

Edward and his brother, Earle

Stinson and Arvie with Edward at their wedding, 1970

Edward and Rachel with Stinson and Arvie at their wedding, 1970

Brian and Susan's wedding, 1976

Brian and Susan's wedding, Edward and Rachel on left, 1976

Sandy, Rachel, Edward, and Edna Rachel, 1978

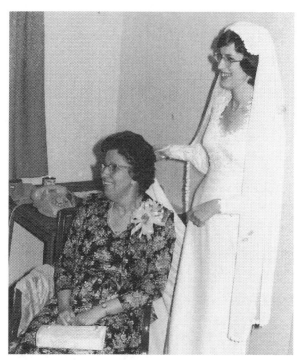

Rachel and Edna Rachel at her wedding, 1978

On our twenty-fifth anniversary

My Darling,

Every tender emotion of the heart and all the joys of living are mingled in every thought of you. These twenty-five years have laid bare before my eyes how profoundly and unreservedly you spoke that day when you uttered those beautiful, frightening words — "All that I am."

As cherished companion of my life you have enriched every aspect of my being immeasurably by submerging your own. You have been all and more than I could ever have dreamed when we began our happy pilgrimage together. I have long been poignantly aware that many of the opportunities, educational and otherwise, which have brought enrichment to my own life were afforded only through your selfless devotion, ever given without the slightest hint that you were aware of the cost to yourself.

And I shall never be able to reveal to you the full measure of my overflowing gratitude that you have been the wonderful mother you have to our children. Again, you have submerged your own life for the sake of theirs. The abiding ideals of Christian character and purpose which we observe with unceasing joy in each of them is more than anything else the fruit of blessed motherhood. Your faithful devotion in mission service and your continuing encouragement in all that

25th anniversary letter from Edward to Rachel

God has given me to be and to do have been to this day the supreme human source of my strength. Whether in the delivery of a sermon, the preparation of a lesson, the experience of prayer, or in just plain living, I am the stronger, the purer, the more satisfied when you are there. With all my heart, I thank my God for you.

And darling, I love you for the brave, cheerful, uncomplaining manner with which you have borne your present illness. God is surely working in His mysterious way for good and for His own glory. I am persuaded that there is some glorious, hidden purpose in all of this which shall yet be revealed and that far beyond your present sufferings there is laid up for you a crown of life.

In a manner more profound than I could have understood twenty-five years ago, I say again with all my heart: "...to have and to hold from this day forward ... in sickness and in health, to love and to cherish, till death do us part...."

In tenderest love, your
Edward

25th anniversary letter, page 2

165

Grandchildren and "granddogs"

Anxious to have grandchildren for many years, Edward and Rachel first had to be satisfied with "granddogs." Neither of them cared for dogs as pets and certainly neither of them was thrilled with the concept of granddogs. They wanted grandchildren! Perhaps because of never being allowed to have dogs as pets when growing up, all three of their children were dog lovers and owned dogs as pets long before they chose to have children of their own. Nevertheless, Edward and Rachel, who usually petted them with the back of a hand or an elbow, tolerated the granddogs.

Between the years of 1978 and 1985, grandchildren finally arrived, and when they did, no words could adequately express their grandparents' joy and excitement. Rachel, Carol and John were born to Stinson and Arvie. Russell and Steven were the sons born to Susan and Brian. Joshua and Elizabeth were the children born to Edna Rachel and Sandy. Each brought unbounded happiness to their grandparents who easily adapted to the role of doting grandparents. Each grandchild received expressive letters of love and appreciation from their grandfather. Visits by any of the grandchildren caused their grandmother's face to light up with expressive happiness. On every visit, each of them immediately went to her for an affectionate embrace, then on to their grandfather for an embrace and one of his special healthy but sweet morsels kept especially for them.

The entire family gathered every year for Rachel's birthday but for Edward and Rachel, it was always more about the grandchildren than her birthday. She, in particular, reveled in the swirling commotion of her grandchildren around her. Both had fond memories of their own grandparents and they hoped to be creating similar memories for their own grandchildren.

Edward's second book, *The Form of Godliness*, published in 1993 was dedicated,

> In grateful memory of my parents
> who cast the mold
> within which these
> thoughts took *form*
>
> and

For my dear grandchildren
with the prayer
that they may
*trans*form them
from words to
life

The book outlined his view of theology and for his grandchildren a testament to the Christian virtues he wished to pass along to them: truth, faith, love and hope. After his diagnosis with terminal cancer in 1999, grandchildren Carol and John wrote to him expressing the hope that one day they too would share their grandfather's understanding and knowledge of God. He found their letters of love and hope meaningful and comforting to him at a particularly difficult time in his life.

Riding in style

After Rachel was diagnosed with multiple sclerosis, the type of vehicle used for doctor appointments, shopping, and church attendance needed to be one that best accommodated her special needs. Initially, the automobile purchased upon arrival in California served the purpose well for it needed only to carry her walker. The time came when she required the use of a wheelchair or needed to have one immediately available should she become overly fatigued when out and about. This required a vehicle with a trunk able to accommodate her wheelchair and therefore, a new vehicle which could do so was purchased.

By the early 1980's, Rachel could not stand or walk on her own and therefore, always required the use of a wheelchair when she left home. Their social lives centered on their church. Services and social activities at church became her most frequent outing. Their next vehicle was a van customized with features to accommodate her wheelchair. It had a hydraulic lift that lifted Rachel in her wheelchair gently into the van. With a raised roof, Edward was able to stand inside to manipulate the wheelchair into position and to secure it beside his seat where she could see forward in the direction they traveled which allowed them to freely converse when riding in it. For the remainder of her life, the van served as their mode of transportation and prevented Rachel from being captive within her own home.

An inventor and innovator

Always looking for ways to improve Rachel's life, Edward used his ingenuity to solve any problem that would make her life easier. His mind was always inquisitive. He designed space-oriented bookracks, nifty little storage areas and a basket for her walker. Searching for solutions to problems, he continuously came up with ingenious contraptions, devices and gadgets. When Rachel could no longer do simple tasks such as point and click a television remote control or hold a book, he devised a stand that was easily pushed away or drawn near to hold those items so that she could use them. He purchased one of the first types of telephone with a speakerphone that allowed her to participate in conversations with family members and friends to hear news of their lives and of the outside world. Their home became a music studio for listening to classical music. He made sure she was able to listen to the music by hanging speakers that were oriented in such a way as to optimize the music for her. Anything he could do to improve her life he set about to do with determination and love.

Spiritual needs

As had been their practice from the beginning of their relationship, Edward and Rachel shared a daily devotional time for Bible study and prayer. Both were important to their relationship, the way in which they lived their lives and as a source of strength as they faced the trials of her illness. Prayer was an especially important aspect of their relationship with one another and with God. How they prayed in light of the circumstances of their lives was testament to their trust and faith in God. How should they pray? More specifically, how should they pray for Rachel? Should they pray for her to walk again? Should they simply pray, seeking God's will for their lives? Their conclusion was that for them, the best way to pray was to order their lives around God's desires so that their very lives became a prayer. They based their conclusion on passages found in the book of Ephesians:

> *With this in mind, then, I kneel in prayer to the Father...that out of the treasures of his glory he may grant you strength and power through his Spirit in your inner being, that through faith Christ may dwell in your hearts love. With deep roots and firm foundations, may you be strong to grasp, with all God's people,*

what is the breadth and length and height and depth of the love of Christ, and to know it., though it is beyond knowledge. So may you attain to the fullness of being the fullness of God Himself.
Ephesians 3:14-19

Praying always with all prayer and supplication in the Spirit, and watching thereunto with all perseverance and supplication for all saints.
Ephesians 6:18

For as long as Rachel could speak, she participated actively. Later, Edward was their voice and went to great lengths to involve her to the extent she comfortably could participate. She looked to him to express her faith, her love for God and her hope for the eternal. Their devotional times were times of companionship. They trusted God and as life companions, they had implicit trust in His plan for their lives as *one*. Their devotional times were times of renewal and times of spiritual growth. Through the reality of their togetherness as *one*, they relied on one another to focus on their own spirituality. Through their shared love and faith, they never lost hope.

A Symphony of Love

Conjugal union is a coming into the fullness of our humanity—however severe the boundaries may become.

Edward and Rachel shared a divine calling and through it a commitment to God in the form of their ministry whether in Nigeria or California. Carrying out the responsibilities of that calling and ministry was their life work. They approached the conclusion of their ministry at Golden Gate with mixed emotions. Edward, who had elected to retire at age sixty-five, would have preferred to continue teaching until mandatory retirement a few years later, but the advancing nature of Rachel's illness precluded any consideration of that option. Yet their ministry was not at an end. Each of them continued their ministry of truth, faith, hope and love and touched people from the many walks of life until the end of their own lives. Seemingly unaware of its far-reaching effects, they assumed a far different kind of ministry in the very way they lived their lives, a ministry that had meaning and purpose for as long as they lived.

Pre-retirement

The years just prior to retirement were difficult ones. Rachel required someone to be with her throughout the day and needed most of Edward's time and attention when he was home. Initially, he hired the wives of seminary students to care for her. During the final two years at Golden Gate, Joanne Stubblefield, a dear friend, lovingly filled their need, staying with Rachel daily while he was in class. Joanne's help went far beyond that of simply staying with Rachel while he was in class; she was a true friend and companion to Rachel, someone he knew was devoted to the loving care she required. Joanne understood their calling, their sense of living as *one*, their faith, and the unique nature of their relationship. She also knew that Edward was determined to care for Rachel for as long as he was able and that no one could quite fill his shoes.

Edward's previous study and research of multiple sclerosis led to his verbalization of a determination to stay as healthy as possible to care for Rachel. He knew she would need him and his ability to care for her and to provide for her needs became an obsession that gave him a strong determination to stay as healthy as he possibly could. Toward that end, he, too, exercised daily and adopted a stringently healthy diet. Walking up a hill to class at a pace few younger men could keep up with or workouts on a treadmill at home kept him physically fit while not reducing his availability to her. Only on rare occasions could someone tempt him with some delicious, unhealthy morsel or in his terms, "mighty delicious victuals." For as long as she lived, he was able to stay, in general, remarkably healthy; however, the limited times of ill health caused him a high level of anxiety while she was alive.

Joanne allowed Edward to fulfill his teaching commitment during the two years she stayed with Rachel. During this time, Rachel began to require more and more of his time, and he came to the realization that he would be unable to carry a full academic teaching load beyond age sixty-five. In May 1983, Edward officially retired from Golden Gate Baptist Theological Seminary.

Deciding where to live

The Humphreys were not able to live in faculty housing once Edward retired. As they faced the agonizing decision of where to live, they considered what was most important to them. Both had legitimate concerns that needed to be factored into the decision. Rachel's limited mobility impeded her ability to make new friends. Their friends were primarily members of their seminary and church families. She had regular scrabble partners who lived nearby that visited often. She was hesitant about moving to a new area where, for a third time, she would be forced to begin anew, only this time with a feeling of isolation brought on by her compromised health and the inability to get around on her own. Edward wanted to write another book and needed access to a theological library.

As they faced this decision, they once again relied on their faith and trust in God as well as a realistic view of the practical details. Well aware of what lay ahead as the symptoms of multiple sclerosis advanced, they knew they required ready access to the medical community wherever they lived. That fact became foremost in their thinking, for they did not own a home and could therefore readily move anywhere without undue financial hardship. The doctors and medical care to which Rachel was accustomed in Marin County made their decision difficult, but, in the end, they decided to move south to San Jose. Their decision was based on the fact that their son, Stinson, was now in medical practice in San Jose. He would be able to facilitate the myriad of necessary contacts in various medical fields that would inevitably be required. As for a library, Edward made the decision he would return to the library at Golden Gate when someone was available to stay with Rachel. They would miss their friends and the familiarity of Marin County, Golden Gate and Tiburon Baptist Church, but they felt they would enjoy the fellowship and opportunities offered by a small community church as they had once done in Nigeria. Last but certainly not least, they would live very near three of their grandchildren—a delightful prospect indeed!

The stress of moving

The spring of 1983 was a busy time. As Edward was preparing to complete his teaching duties, he prepared to vacate his office. Bookcases filled with his books needed to be packed. His personality was such that he was determined not to delay for a moment whoever was moving into the office he was leaving. The same was true at home. A new faculty member would be moving into their apartment on Platt Court and he would be the one to pack most of their belongings and prepare for the move to San Jose. As the semester concluded, final exam papers required grading. Perhaps more than he realized or was willing to admit, Edward was fatigued and felt the stress of the impending move.

The previous twelve months had already been unusually stressful and particularly difficult. One morning, Rachel slept well past the time she was usually awake. Initially, Edward did not want to disturb her, feeling she must need the extra sleep. By midmorning, however, he was worried and decided it best to call one of his children whose expertise he routinely relied upon. Stinson's advice was to awaken her but when Edward attempted to do so, he found her difficult to arouse and incoherent. An ambulance was immediately called but by the time it arrived, he had taken her temperature and found it was 107 degrees! Evaluation in the emergency room of Marin General Hospital revealed pneumonia. He was then told what he was not prepared to hear. Rachel might not survive. He had never heard anything like that before and felt, as he later said, "as if the walls of the room were closing in on (him)." He simply was not at a point that allowed him to imagine life without his darling. She slowly recovered from a chemical pneumonia, the result of unknowingly aspirating one of her medications. The event had taken its toll on Edward by the time it came to move.

The tables turned in the weeks ahead. One evening, as moving day approached, Edward and Rachel enjoyed some pizza, not a usual part of their normally healthy diet. After their daily devotional, he readied her for bed but then as he prepared for bed, he suspected something might be amiss. Ostensibly, because they had eaten pizza earlier and he felt unusually fatigued, he discounted for the time being what he felt in his chest. Recounting the episode later, he recalled having discomfort in his chest that he described as heartburn or indigestion. Whatever it was, he was concerned enough to leave the front door to their apartment unlocked in case she needed to call someone who would then need access to the apartment. He called no one to report the symptoms he felt and said nothing to Rachel, but it would not be long before he discovered he should have.

When moving day arrived, seminary students came to help with packing and loading of the Humphreys' belongings into a rental truck. Edward worked alongside them, never mentioning to anyone what had happened the night he had left the door unlocked. It was not until after they had settled into their home in San Jose that he first mentioned the episode. In his mind, anything Rachel needed came first and she needed to establish a relationship with a new physician as soon as possible after moving.

Moving to San Jose brought the expected burst of activity. They needed to unpack, to learn their way around and to establish a new church home. Rachel saw her new physician almost immediately. Edward would become a patient of the same physician only much sooner than he had anticipated. Before he did, however, he very much wanted to get a new vegetable garden established. Now that he had the time, he wanted to capitalize on his years of farming experience.

Back to farming

The home, into which the Humphreys moved, had a backyard large enough for a vegetable garden. Edward decided to erect raised beds for his vegetable garden. Each day, he rolled Rachel out onto the back porch in her wheel chair to enjoy the sunshine while he worked. The two talked, reminisced, laughed, and told stories. They were happy and had adjusted well to living within their new community. Perhaps retirement was not so bad after all! It had been a long time since they had been able to spend day after day together, and they relished every moment. Conversation turned to activities they would enjoy, plans for his new book, and inevitably their grandchildren. They were in love and enjoyed one another's company as much as they had for the almost forty years of marriage. At Wake Forest, they had dreamed bold dreams of working in Africa; now they were able to relive their dreams come true.

Although he exercised regularly, it had been some time since Edward had been involved in manual labor. He struggled with the large boards he had purchased to build the raised beds for his garden and worked tirelessly to bring wheelbarrows of top soil from the driveway to the backyard. That was when he noticed it; the uncomfortable tightness in his chest was unmistakable. Temporarily forgetting about the pizza episode, he casually mentioned the feeling of tightness in his chest to Stinson who had fortuitously stopped by to visit. Now that Edward had more uncommitted time, he agreed to seek medical attention. His desire was to stay as healthy as possible in his determination to take care of his darling for as long as she needed him.

A temporary interruption

Within a day or two, Edward was ready for coronary artery bypass surgery. He had seen his new physician, who recommended a cardiologist, who helped him remember the pizza episode, had miserably failed a treadmill stress test, and had an angiogram that showed advanced coronary artery disease, consulted with the cardiac surgeon and was now waiting with Stinson before heading to the operating room. Rachel was safely in the loving care of Susan and Edna Rachel. Both had dropped everything in their lives to be with her. They had young children, were working in high stress nursing occupations but when needed were available to those who had taught them the meaning of love. When the orderly arrived, Edward asked if they could pray. He had much to be thankful for, and his prayer that morning was one of praise and thanksgiving. Feeling confident in the outcome, he was ready to go to the operating room.

Edward had tenderly kissed Rachel good-bye before he left home for the hospital. It was a scene witnessed by their children many times before. Each spoke lovingly as they gazed wistfully into one another's eyes. He told her he would be "good as new" when he saw her again. Rachel was at peace. Her trust and faith in God gave her assurance all would be well.

Rachel insisted on going to the coronary intensive care unit to see Edward after his surgery. The moment was sweet and tender, a moment in which no words were necessary to convey their boundless love. She did not stay long but wanted to see Edward and see for herself that he was okay. Left to themselves, they looked absorbed in the tender embrace of one another's love. Rachel, unable to leave her wheelchair, and Edward, unable to leave his bed, nevertheless seemed oblivious to their surroundings. If only for a few moments, they looked to be caught up in the mere presence of one another. After telling him, she loved him and smiling broadly, she was wheeled from the unit, only able to contain the tears until outside the door. The tears that flowed were tears of joy. Those few moments had stirred deep emotion within Rachel. Edward was doing well.

A joyful homecoming awaited Edward when he arrived at home from Good Samaritan Hospital. Susan and Edna Rachel now had two patients to care for. Edward eagerly wanted to return to caring for Rachel as soon as possible, but recognized the need to recover, go to rehab, and regain his strength. Rachel was satisfied just to have him home. He was temporarily unable to care for her but he recovered quickly. Their hearts were filled with joy, their hope fulfilled and their faith sustained by God through the unexpected ordeal.

New priorities

Priorities changed after Edward's narrow escape from the potentially serious consequences of heart disease. He was able to put in a garden later that summer, but he went about it at a more deliberate and controlled pace. Once the garden was in place, seeded, and thriving, he set about the task of converting a spare bedroom into his study. In his usual self-sufficient manner, he went about the task of building and installing his own bookshelves.

Even with her gradual decline in health, it was difficult for Rachel to sit idly by, but the ravages of multiple sclerosis had taken their toll. Although she never voiced complaint, she was unable to be active and involved. Nevertheless, God used her in ways that did not require an active life. Her sweet disposition in the face of profound disability became an inspiration to all who knew her. Never did she give voice to bitterness. Never did she lose faith and hope. Often she expressed hope for a cure for multiple sclerosis, telling everyone a cure was "just around the corner." Displaying an ongoing optimism, she frequently told her grandchildren she would walk again one day. Visits by the grandchildren brought certain brightness and joy to her life.

When Edward was back on his feet and had recovered from bypass surgery, they began looking for a new church home in earnest. When they first moved to San Jose, they had spent their Sundays visiting several Baptist churches in the area. Many of the pastors already knew Edward. Some had been his students at Golden Gate. He had known others from prior speaking engagements while he was at Golden Gate.

Settling into a routine

Ultimately, Edward and Rachel decided to join a small church within the community in which they lived. Camden Avenue Baptist Church became their new home away from home, and its members became like family. They had wanted to join a church that they could support and contribute to rather than one that would be solely supportive of them. They felt they had discovered a church in which there was mutual support. Whatever they did throughout their lives, they did to serve God, and this church, they felt, served Him best. Over the ensuing years, Edward and Rachel did what they could to support their church. A time came when the pastor was unable to afford to repair his car. They had both the van and a sedan, so they did what, for them, came natural and loaned the pastor their car indefinitely. Church members became loving friends, visiting frequently, offering companionship, bringing a cassette tape recording of the service on Sundays when the Humphreys were unable to attend so that Edward and Rachel could hear what they had missed.

Although he was retired, Edward still managed to stay very busy. Serving as Rachel's primary caregiver was a full-time job. Nevertheless, he found the time to run the errands, do household chores, build dollhouses for his granddaughters, garden, write a book, and always look for ways to make Rachel's life more comfortable. His life rotated around hers. By necessity, hers was dependent on him. She passed her days reading, doing her crewel art, listening to the classical music they both loved, and watching her favorite television shows. Her last crewel piece was finished in 1985. As she tried to complete it, she lost all dexterity in her hands, and a loving friend had to help her struggle with the very last of it. As the months passed, her life became increasingly more confined and constrained but inevitably, her spirits remained high.

The Humphreys had many close friends in Nigeria and California. For many, San Jose was now on the map, particularly their home on Standish Drive. Friends came to visit or spend the day. Some came to spend a night or two. Each brought love and joy as their friends brought the outside world to them. Former missionaries, seminary colleagues, Nigerian friends, students from both seminaries in which they served, former Scrabble partners and family, all came to visit. Siblings from both sides of the family visited from North Carolina. All brought love. Some brought a bit of the past. All blessed them with the very nature of the kindness shown by their visit.

Home sweet home

Uprooting moves had been frequent for the Humphreys. Over the course of their life together, they had moved often, but each time they had adapted easily to their new home. The home in San Jose was their last, and it suited their needs well. The home had room for overnight guests who were frequent. A study and a workbench in the garage were important to Edward.

Before they moved to San Jose, Edward began using a hydraulic lift to move Rachel safely and comfortably from her bed into her recliner, and when needed, to bathroom facilities. The lift required a great deal of room to manipulate properly and safely. Therefore, he set about the task of making room to maneuver the lift safely with her in it. He put in a doublewide door to their bedroom, which provided easy access for her wheelchair and room to move the lift about. She had hoped to be able to use a motorized wheelchair, but it was never a reality, for when she got one, she no longer had the dexterity in her hands to use it. Bathing proved to be a long-term problem for Rachel. On Platt Court, she had problems falling in the shower and adjusting the water temperature. She was no longer able to use a shower and needed a bathtub by the time they moved to San Jose. Edward raised the bathtub to waist height in order to facilitate giving her a bath. The time came soon enough when she required a bed bath, but he intended to give her a bath in a bathtub for as long as possible.

Music of love and love of music

"...(music) is to the soul what a water bath is to the body." ~ Oliver Wendell Holmes.

Music was always a part of Edward and Rachel's home. Both of them were passionate about listening to classical music, particularly the violin and Beethoven. In Nigeria, they listened to music on a shortwave radio. They upgraded to a stereo system when they were at Golden Gate. After retirement, they purchased a complete music system, which was setup throughout the house. As an avid reader and music lover, she listened to music as she read. As a lifelong student, he listened to music as he studied. They often began playing music in the early morning soon after they awoke. They listened as he helped her with resistance exercises and physical therapy. On many days, it played throughout the day. Music was usually the first sound visitors heard as they approached the front door. They left having witnessed a tender love story and the union of two souls whose love played harmoniously the melodies of a grand and glorious symphony.

The Music Crescendos

In the commonalities of life with my dear one, soul became knit with soul. And there, I was awakened to a new sense of the beauty of divine truth, the exceeding tenderness of divine love, the quiet tranquility of divine peace, and the abiding comfort and joy of divine hope.

As was his usual custom, Edward wrote Rachel a love letter to commemorate their forty-fifth wedding anniversary. Each year he sought to write a letter that expressed his most tender and deepest emotions, a beautiful and eloquent expression of love from his heart. Each year he read the letter aloud to her and each year it was a special time of sharing that she looked forward to with great anticipation for in her own way, through the expressiveness of her eyes, she had the ability to capture and hold him enwrapped in her love. The letter he read on May 23, 1992 would be the last he read to her for their love, their symphony, would play on "unfinished" by their forty-sixth anniversary. He concluded the letter writing,

> *Like the well-integrated composition of a majestic symphony with its varied, often complex, and recurring themes, this love is bound up with all of the components of that life which we have actually experienced together. Whether the focus is upon long-cherished dreams or lost opportunities, perceived achievements or known failures, good health or devastating illness, this love encompasses and embraces them all, believing that even the minor notes, which intrude upon our harmony, can but lend exquisite and haunting beauty to the whole composition. For after all, the most captivating strains of a great symphony are more often than not the adagio with its subdued, slow-moving sometimes thinly veiled hint of underlying pain or unrelieved sorrow."*

The ravages of multiple sclerosis

Over the years, Rachel endured the ravages of multiple sclerosis with uncommon dignity and grace. She did so with absolute trust in divine love, with the comfort of divine hope and with resolute faith. Frequently asked about the outward appearance of no resentment or bitterness, she responded by saying that she lived one day at a time and whatever happened to her was in God's hands. Her answer carried a certain validity and depth of meaning that left the inquirer thoroughly convinced it represented her true feelings. Family members received an identical response. She had given the same answer before she knew a diagnosis. Her answer was remarkable in light of the extent to which she suffered with the disease and undoubtedly, she served as an inspiration to all who knew her.

For the nine years Rachel resided in San Jose, she lived trapped in a body with little sensation, awkward movement and crippling dysfunction, ultimately unable to move any part of her body except her head. Swallowing became increasingly difficult until it became dangerous for fear of aspiration. The last five years of her life, she was fed through a tube in her abdomen (gastrostomy). Speech was strained, then whispered, finally inaudible and ultimately her lips used to form the words she wished to communicate. Her bodily functions resulted first in occasional accidents, later required diapers, and ultimately required Edward's assistance. Breathing became labored, then deep breaths became impossible, and for almost the last three years of her life, her breathing was through a tube in her trachea (tracheotomy). Over the course of time, she developed multiple symptoms, including weakness, clumsiness, fatigue, numbness, spasticity, phantom limb pain, tingling, burning sensations, tremors, and loss of fine muscle control. When she lost control of her muscles of facial expression, she was no longer able to smile voluntarily. Some of the secondary symptoms and problems often associated with the disease, such as bladder infections and bedsores, never affected her, which was directly attributable to the level of care Edward provided.

In spite of all these problems, as unbelievable as it may seem, she never gave voice to anger, bitterness or resentment. Her faith in God remained a constant throughout her life.

Love conquers all

One Mother's Day, a day on which Edward always dressed Rachel in one of her prettiest dresses, the family assembled for pictures after church. No matter what the occasion, she was happiest when her family was around. Repeatedly, the family urged her to smile, but her lips could no longer form a smile. She had slowly lost control of the muscles used for facial expression and simply could no longer show emotion by smiling. Quietly and gently, Edward told the others what he already knew. She had learned to smile with her eyes.

Awkwardly, Rachel struggled to form with her lips the words "thank you" and "I love you." Her eyes became expressive, dancing with delight when grandchildren came to visit and for Edward her eyes were expressive of the most heartfelt love for him. Regarding her ability to communicate her love, he wrote

> *"If I had to specify the 'high road' of our union, one with the other, it would surely have to be the span of time … when physical strength had failed and only love remained. Long after she had lost the ability to speak with an audible voice or to voluntarily move her limbs, she would fervently form with her lips those immortal words, 'I love you.' And I could read in her lovely, limpid, expressive eyes the 'forever and ever' of a love that is now eternal."*

Rachel and Edward, 1992

Tortured decisions

With each downturn in Rachel's health, they faced burdensome, tortured decisions. She had long been at peace with her mortality and at times expressed verbally her readiness to go Home, according to His plan. At times, she openly longed for the ultimate healing nature of death, for she was confident in her faith and trust in God. Edward understood her feelings but was not ready for her to go simply to make his life less difficult. Indeed, those last two years of her life were, he wrote,

> *...without compare in the whole of our lives in union one with the other. In those years, we discovered more deeply than in all the others what it means to be sweethearts, what it means to be one before God ... It was all the culmination of all that heart could desire or memory hold dear. In giving me Rachel to complete my life in this world, God's grace was superabundant! Only heaven can exceed what it bequeathed to me.*

In the late spring of 1989, before Rachel had her tracheotomy performed, she developed a very high respiratory rate and labored breathing one Sunday afternoon. Rushed to Good Samaritan Hospital in San Jose, it was discovered that she had developed a life-threatening pneumonia and was critically ill. After she was stabilized in the emergency room, the physician came to speak with Edward and Stinson. In sudden, certain, and shocking terms, he asked them for instructions about efforts to resuscitate her. Crestfallen, Edward turned pale with the realization of making a decision he had done everything in his power to avoid. He knew the correct answer from Rachel's viewpoint. It was clear what the physician expected the answer to be. It was almost more than he could bear to agree with orders for "DNR" (Do Not Resuscitate). Immediately, he asked for a moment in private with his son, but he knew what the answer had to be. Alone, the two bowed their heads. As tears filled their eyes, they turned to God. No one knew if the orders were ever to be carried out, but they had to be given.

Rachel made a remarkable recovery. Overjoyed, Edward took her home with renewed vigor and passion for life. A few weeks later, they happily celebrated their anniversary. The music played on. Nevertheless, they faced one last burdensome decision. The only hope of avoiding repeated bouts of pneumonia lay with performing a tracheotomy. If she agreed, a tube would be placed in her trachea to facilitate breathing and provide access for suctioning to keep her lungs clear. Her physician felt it would prolong her life; however, she would have to learn to speak again by closing off the artificial trachea manually, which would allow her to speak only in whispered tones, if at all. Rachel's immediate reaction was to avoid it. Just as quickly, Edward encouraged her to have it done. It was a monumental decision that involved the entire family. Everyone had something to say, and everyone urged her to have it done. Yet she continued to vacillate, questioning whether she should attempt to prolong her life or not. She did not want to be a burden to her family. Only after her daughter-in-law, Arvie, told her it was important for her to live long enough for her grandchildren to know and remember her did she become comfortable with the decision to proceed. She had never been able to do the sort of things that grandmothers especially enjoyed. She was not able to pick them up to hold them close, nor could she enjoy many of the expressions of love most grandmothers do, but now there was a way to show them the extent of her love. She grabbed the opportunity. At the time of her death, her grandchildren ranged from seven to fourteen years of age. Each knew her, remembered her, and loved her.

Devoted caregiver

Edward cared for Rachel in every way he could and was able. He learned routine nursing skills, became an expert dietician, a physical therapist and for the last few years of her life, he became an around-the-clock intensive care nurse. He dressed her, bathed her, brushed her hair, flossed and brushed her teeth. He helped her with stretching, resistance exercises and physical therapy to prevent contractures or scarring of muscles and tendons that would have otherwise resulted in severe deformity. He prepared their meals, cut her food and eventually learned to prepare nutritious liquefied meals to feed her through her gastrostomy feeding tube. He developed recipes that he called "formulas" that provided nutritious liquid meals combining baby food, especially meats, eggs, fruit, juice, milk, and liquid vitamins. He kept a supply mixed together in the refrigerator, ready to place in the feeding bag, which he always hung to drip through the tube before he sat down to eat his own meals. He kept the feeding tube and bag as well as the gastrostomy site on her abdomen clean and infection-free for the five years she had it in place. He used the hydraulic lift to move her from the bed to her recliner, from the recliner to her portable toilet chair, and from her recliner back to bed. He did that numerous times each day. He massaged her spastic muscles that often twitched and he rubbed lotion over her body to keep her skin soft and free of bedsores. For almost three years, he suctioned her tracheotomy breathing tube to keep it and her lungs free of mucous. He learned to listen for her coughing, even when sleeping. When he heard the coughing, he would quickly get up to suction her trachea and lungs through the breathing tube. For almost two years, he did this throughout the night every night, often getting only two to three hours of sleep each night. He performed every conceivable task of day-to-day living while also providing advanced and skilled nursing care.

Edward also went to the market, cleaned the house, and did the laundry. They refused outside help, for they wanted to reserve their enjoyment of life and one another for themselves. He consistently refused to allow Rachel to enter a nursing home—a promise they had made to one another many years before her condition had become that of an invalid. He read to her, kept a hummingbird feeder filled where she could watch the birds come and go, brought as much of the outside world to her as possible, and listened to music with her. His life revolved around hers. Hers revolved within his. Her life was his to live for. She lived for him. They lived as *one* in every way.

The last two years

Edward and Rachel's lives became increasingly confined after the tracheotomy. With adeptness, he easily learned how to suction her trachea correctly, to keep it clear of mucous that collected and to perform necessary suctioning to keep her lungs clear. He also learned how to change the tracheotomy tube and keep it clean. She never had another bout of pneumonia or pulmonary infection of any kind. Undoubtedly, he was able to add many months of joy and love to her life. He found the time more precious than ever, giving his life completely to her care. Unselfishly, he lived in every way for her. She now required around-the-clock nursing care, and he was determined to provide it himself. And he did! With very little sleep each night, he somehow managed to function with a clear mind, always performing each task with a high level of expertise. Nevertheless, the family began to worry about his health and encouraged him to allow a nurse's aide to help him during the day. He never relented in his determination to be the principal caregiver for his darling, but ultimately allowed a nurse's aide to help with some of her personal hygiene. She enjoyed the contact with the outside world and it gave him a much needed break.

In those last years together, when he rose in the morning, Edward turned on music before he took a quick shower. Helping Rachel with her stretching and resistance exercises came next, after which he would give her the liquid meals he had prepared the night before. Only then did he allow himself time to quickly eat breakfast. Next, he transferred her to her recliner using the lift, cleaned up the kitchen, made beds, and prepared her meals for the following day; always staying one day ahead lest something happen that prevented him from preparing them. Only then, if there was time, did he allow himself the luxury of retreating to his study to read and reflect quietly. Lunch came next, and once again, Rachel received hers first. They then took a brief afternoon nap unless they had visitors or some need interfered. The remainder of the afternoon and early evening he spent reading to her, listening to music, or simply spending time together before he began the process of getting her ready for bed. His evening meal was always cereal, while she received her formula. Together they had their devotional time with Bible reading and prayer. He then used the lift to move her to bed as he had done throughout the day to move her about. He was aware that moving her several times during the day helped prevent bedsores. Once she was in bed, he massaged the muscles in her limbs and rubbed lotion on her skin. Seemingly, never-ending suctioning of her trachea interrupted each activity. When he eventually turned out the light, he kissed her, told her he loved her, and then let her sleep while he prepared for the next day. Each day was full—full of love, happiness, and joy.

The only break Edward allowed himself was to run his errands and do the necessary shopping when someone could be there with Rachel. Each family member visited often, which allowed him time to shop, bank, and take care of other necessary functions of daily life outside the home. One of these, Stinson's mother-in-law, Betty Oody, came every week to wash and style Rachel's hair, give her a manicure, and visit with her. Each time they compared thoughts about their mutual grandchildren. Each time, Edward never failed to tell Rachel that she was beautiful, that she was his darling and that he loved her.

The family was worried about Edward's health and concerned that he would not be able to sustain the demands he placed upon himself.

Rachel was tired, tired of holding on. She had watched her grandchildren grow to well-adjusted children full of life, love, and happiness. She had enjoyed each of their visits, their hugs (although she could not hug them) and had been thrilled as she listened to what they told her about school and activities in their lives. Yet there came a time when she was clearly ready to go Home. She was trapped in a body that, to her, had lost all usefulness. Increasingly, she longed to look upon the face of God.

The symphony plays on—unfinished

Rachel's downhill course had been gradual throughout the course of her illness. Each step in her debilitation seemed to come gradually to those who loved her most and were often around her. As she approached the last of her earthly journey, she did so tranquilly, perhaps knowing she would soon be free of the constraints that had ravaged her body in the form of multiple sclerosis. Before she slipped into a comatose state a few hours before she died, she seemed particularly enraptured by contact with loved ones. By chance, her son, Stinson, stopped by for a visit hours before she lost consciousness. He was struck by the intensity in which she held him in her gaze. Her eyes were so unusually bright and expressive that he left thinking that she seemed more communicative than she had in quite some time. It was the last time he saw his mother before she entered a state of deep unconsciousness. As he left that evening, Stinson noted that, as usual, music was playing in the background, this time, Beethoven's Symphony No. 5 in C minor. As always, however, the music that played in the foreground was the impassioned strains of a love story, the music of his parents' love for one another.

Edward and Rachel enjoyed music more than any other form of entertainment. They listened to it on the radio, on their music system and often watched concerts on television. Music was their love, and their love was music. Years after Rachel was no longer with him, Edward used musical terms to express his feelings about their love, writing,

> *There came for us a time in our togetherness when we were acutely conscious of the receding motion of the familiar world. Years gave way to months, months to weeks, weeks to days, days to hours, and hours to moments—and then, except for the precious gift of memory (and our blessed hope!), the story of our*

temporal togetherness was at an end. The lovely symphony that had been in formation for nearly half a century was brought to its temporal terminus—'unfinished.' And that was inevitable, for that lovely melody must employ an immortal language and a heavenly harmony with which, alone, it can be brought to its grand and glorious finale.

Rachel died quietly and peacefully during the evening hours of October 24, 1992. At her side, Edward "lingered there for a time at the border between the temporal and the eternal and pondered in the depths of (his) soul the meaning of both life and death." He then "bent low for one last tender embrace...and kissed the cheeks that had long been for (him) the fairest earthly reflection of the radiant light of God."

An Unfinished Symphony

Conjugal love, like music, has wider power through its
varying tempos and its major and minor keys.

Rachel was remembered foremost for her commitment to God and to His service. Her devotion to Edward was intertwined with their call to a life of ministry before Him. She lived the life promised on the inscription she placed within his wedding band, "All That I Am." As a wife, she was that ideal of purity, grace and sweetness which had been the substance of his highest and holiest dreams. As a mother, she loved and nurtured her children in a way that engendered their desire to emulate her own life. As a grandmother, through an act of selfless love, she allowed her grandchildren to know and love her. To her friends, she was an example of grace, faith and optimism in the face of unimaginable adversity.

Rachel never complained about her long illness, and, in doing so, sustained those about her. Multiple Sclerosis was not a fate she chose, rather, a fate she accepted. She always bore the suffering it caused with a cheerful, patient, and sweet disposition. The manner in which she lived became a veritable example of trust, faith, love and hope.

On Rachel's journey through life, she traveled an unknown road, encountering greater obstacles than most. In her struggle to reach the end, she relied on her Shepherd to lead her through nourishing pastures to restore her soul. There He made her lie down in peace "beside the still waters," under His watchful eye. Day by day, it was His presence and His loving care that provided that peace. In Christian fellowship, she embodied the essence of faith. In life, she provided a glimpse of a saint-in-the-making. Through the mercy of God, she found the spiritual strength to reach the end of her journey, the soul of a saint. (Adapted from an article entitled, "Beside the Still Waters," by Edward Humphrey, a paraphrase of the twenty-third Psalm)

Remembering

On Christmas Eve in 1946, Edward sent Rachel a profoundly prophetic letter. In anticipation of their wedding day in the coming spring, he wrote,

> *I hope that one day we shall look back across the years through which we shall have come together and see that though there has been a comingling of the sad with the sweet, of the sorrowful with the joyful, we have endured as one soul, receiving all our strength from an all-wise and loving Father. And may we see in our wake a touch of 'beauty where there were ashes, and garments of praise where there was the spirit of heaviness.' Rachel, I think that we shall then look into the dimmed eyes of the other and read meanings too deep for tears, and then together lift our tired but happy faces even unto the face of God to catch the full splendor of Eternal grace.*

Almost forty-six years later, when announcing Rachel's death, Edward discovered that previous missive and in a letter to friends wrote:

> *I fancy that with unhindered vision she has indeed beheld 'the full splendor of Eternal grace.' As a helpless invalid for many years, she waited patiently and uncomplainingly for the moment of her glorious translation. Now it has come, and she is forever with our blessed Lord.*

One of the first personal letters Edward wrote following Rachel's death was to his grandchildren. In it, he expressed for her many of the feelings she had longed to express herself. She had been unable to do so, for by the time they reached the age to comprehend the extent of what she wished to tell them, she could no longer speak. Undoubtedly, the inability to engage her grandchildren in meaningful conversation was one of the greatest disappointments in her life.

Edward and Rachel with all their grandchildren, 1989.

Three generations—Edward, John, and Stinson, 1987

October 29, 1992

Dear Rachel, Russell, Carol, Steven, Joshua, John and Elizabeth,

When Grandmother went home to be with God, there were still many things, which she wanted to say to each of you, but could not. Three or four years ago, she tried to make a tape recording for each of you describing her own happy childhood and family background, her early school days, and her walk with God. She wanted to tell you about the birth and early childhood of each of her dear children (your parents) and of the great joy, which each one of them brought to her as they developed from childhood to adolescence to adulthood. But to her great and lasting dismay, the recorder could no longer pick up the frail sound of her voice. The fact that she could not now pass these intimate details on to you remained for her an indescribable disappointment until the very end of her life.

She loved each one of you very dearly and was movingly proud to be your grandmother. When each one of you was born, she literally put her whole heart and soul into the stitching of a birth sampler to mark that wonderful event. The last of these were accomplished with amazing determination, for she had already lost the dexterity of both hands and could maneuver her needle with only the most persistent effort. When the last one was completed, the happy look of triumph beamed from her lovely face.

During the final months of her life, she would look forward wistfully to each visit which you made and wanted so badly to engage you in conversation concerning the things which were of absorbing interest to you. But as you know, she could only sit in silence. I know that this was exceedingly painful to her; and it must surely have been so to you as well.

I do wish that you each could have known her in the full bloom of health; none of you have ever known her except as an invalid. In the "unbiased" opinion of your granddaddy, she was the most beautiful, the most elegant, the most charming, and the most lovely creature who ever walked the face of the earth.

Remember her as one who loved her family with a love as broad and as deep as life itself and in this context, "family" includes not only her children and her husband, but her grandchildren as well. While I am on the subject, let me just add: "So do I."

With all my love and prayers,

Granddaddy Humphrey

Letter from Edward to his grandchildren, October 1992

Adjustment to life without Rachel

Preparation for their time of separation began months before it actually occurred. Edward and Rachel made the necessary end-of-life decisions together. He was grateful he did not face them without her. The memorial service for Rachel took place a few days after her death and the long, painful time of adjustment to life without her began. For the years during which her care consumed his daily life, it was his fervent hope and prayer that he would be able to complete the task. With his hopes fulfilled, it now seemed he might be at a loss with too much time on his hands, but shortly, he delved into writing a flurry of letters to family and friends followed by time visiting with each of his children and his brother Earle. Then he was off to North Carolina to visit both his and Rachel's siblings and in particular, his eldest sister Frances, struggling with cancer. When he returned, he set about making the final preparations required to publish his second book, *The Form of Godliness.*

The ministry continues

The Form of Godliness gave Edward the means to express his own view of theology. As a Christian, he felt that his thinking and his very life must be undertaken responsibly before God. In great depth, he discussed these thoughts in this book, laying out four principal Christian virtues: truth, faith, love and hope. These virtues were his foundation as he sought to live his life in the very form of godliness about which he wrote. In everything he did, including caring for Rachel, he felt he was serving God. He viewed all of life through his relationship with God, seeing holiness in ordinary, everyday experiences.

Edward was a natural caregiver. He based his life on service to others and was grateful that God had given him the strength and health to give Rachel his all. And so, he set about the task of finding and helping others in need. Hospice had provided the Humphreys with valuable services such as the required mixing of some of her medications as well as relieving him of some routine hygiene tasks. Always grateful for the help he received, he found others in need and offered his own service. One was an elderly couple forced to live apart for reasons of age and health. A stroke left the husband with limitations beyond his wife's capabilities to care for him. Sympathizing with their situation, Edward gladly offered to provide transportation, taking her to run errands and to visit her husband regularly at his nursing home. Patiently, Edward would wait for as many hours as the wife wanted to visit with her husband, before taking her home. For as long as Edward lived, he looked for similar situations. His own life represented the very form of godliness about which he had written.

Consciousness of God

With more time to study, Edward found peace, quiet, and reflective solitude among his books. He now had as much time as he wanted to study and read. No longer constrained by obligations at home, he became involved leading seminars at his church and frequently filled in for pastors on Sundays at surrounding churches in the area. He developed a special relationship with Aptos Baptist Church in Aptos, California. Stinson's father-in-law, Gene Oody, its pastor for several years, was Edward's close friend for over three decades. With a natural common bond and mutual interests, the two men appreciated one another's company and discussed a wide range of topics. Inevitably, the conversation turned toward theological discussions. Gene regarded Edward as a "true friend and Christian brother."

Most of Edward's study time was spent engaged in his life-long quest to understand his own spiritual nature as it related to his thinking and understanding of God. Indeed, he sought to live responsibly before God and to live a godly life. He often led seminars and discussion groups at his church and others, which gave him the occasion to delve further within himself and his own spirituality. Often at the conclusion of one of these seminars, he mused aloud that perhaps he benefitted more from his preparation than did those who attended. Edward's own intellect never hindered his respect and appreciation for the views of others. His patience gave him the ability to discuss topics of a spiritual nature with great humility. The Bible was one such topic. On one occasion, he led a seminar on the Bible and said, "For at best, I consider myself only a beginner in the understanding of important matters of the Christian faith." He approached the Bible with an "eager openness to the leadership and control of the Holy Spirit" and with "faithfulness to all that has been gained in conscious encounters with God through exposure to the biblical message." Throughout life, he undertook an "arduous study of the Bible itself," but felt that a full understanding did not lie within his grasp for he was "still of this earth."

Edward regarded family as one of the dearest of God's gifts to humankind and felt it to be among the richest of human treasures. He wrote, "The Christian family, based on marriage, offers unique ground for the development and nurturance of character, independent thought and life. From it, family values, priorities, ideals, grace, joy and truth emanate from two lives that flow as one stream."

A conscious experience of God dated from Edward's early childhood. Godly parents taught him the meaning of responsibility to God, to his parents, to his family and to his neighbors. He could not remember a time when he was "oblivious to the presence and claim of God" upon his life. In his relationship with God, there was a distinction between the objective and the subjective. Both were always present and essential, but the primary was the objective, for God was always present, always real. The subjective was also always present but highly variable for it was manifest in the character of his humanity. His personal faith was assured in the reality of divine grace.

The music of love

In May 1993, on what would have been Edward and Rachel's forty-sixth wedding anniversary, he began writing what he termed an annual "Soliloquy on an Unfinished Symphony" in the place of the usual anniversary letter. Their life together had been a sojourn in which they continually discovered the range and depth of the sacred vows they had taken at the altar of marriage. It made a beautiful story of love, one that Edward wrote, "...can never be adequately transcribed from heart to parchment: Mortal language is much too frail for such exalted usage; and mere words, however elegantly chosen, are in this context, scarcely more than empty symbols." Nevertheless, he continued to write the soliloquies annually on the date of his wedding anniversary and in his own words began to tell the story of the love that had been theirs. [See Appendix B]

It was important for Edward to have a place to go after Rachel was no longer with him physically. He went regularly to the cemetery and spent hours alone with his thoughts that were filled with precious memories. The time gave him a sense of connection for they were inseparably *one* throughout their earthly existence and remained inseparably *one* through this brief time apart. His thoughts were of a love written in his heart as a beautiful and lovely melody, a melody that now played on to the accompaniment of a heavenly chorus of love. For him, their love was akin to a musical symphony, a symphony that continued to play on, unfinished.

With hope, he endured. With faith, he was sustained. With love, he lived.

One Word More

Love is...majestic in its freedom to be just what it is—an unhindered reaching out to others....(for) neither freedom nor love can be what it is in separation one from the other. Freedom is the absolute condition of love; love is the absolute measure of freedom.

Throughout his life, Edward was especially fond of poetry. He had been exposed to it very early in life when listening to his father read in cadence some of the great Scottish, English and American poetry. Rachel gave him several of the great books of poetry over the years and shared his love of poetry. He was fond of a wide range of poetry but the collection of fifty poems by Robert Browning published under the superscription "Men and Women," the last of which was a poem entitled "One Word More" was his favorite. Browning, throughout the first forty-nine poems included numerous expressions of love for his wife, Elizabeth Barrett Browning, but in the end, could never be satisfied that he had adequately expressed his love to her or the essence of those most tender emotions for her that lay within his heart. Hence the final composition, "One Word More." Edward referred to it often, using the words of its title frequently in his writing, seminars and speaking engagements.

Edward had a special love affair with words, becoming a master at expressing his thoughts with carefully chosen words. With elegant beauty and formal eloquence, he used words to write in such a way that they fairly leapt from a written page and always, there was a place for "one word more," especially in matters of the heart. Therefore, after Rachel's death, each of his children urged him to write about his life and in particular his life with her. For a brief time he began to tell his story of love. For him, it was a story of ever-deepening love, of uninterrupted love. It was a story of love that, in the last years of earthly life with Rachel, could only be communicated heart-to-heart. It was a story he never finished writing. His attempt to tell his story of love would never be complete for there always remained another phrase, another expression, another word to convey the beauty and nature of his love for Rachel.

Edward's love story never lay dormant within his heart for his memory of life with Rachel increasingly rested in the joyful hope of a heavenly harmony. It was a story of sweethearts and a story of their love as *one* before God. The story he began to tell took the form of his annual soliloquy on an unfinished symphony, written each year on his wedding anniversary in memory of Rachel. With words of rhyme and prose, he began by writing,

> *My heart knows a dear story of love*
> *A love that can never die*
> *And my heart is acquainted with grief,*
> *A grief that would rob love of*
> *Its fairest human prize*
> *But my heart finds solace in a blessed hope*
> *A hope that reaches beyond the*
> *Farthest tentacles of grief*

> *And so, a beautiful symphony lies 'unfinished' for frail finite language could never grasp the climactic strains of that lovely theme. These must await, meanwhile, the facility of an immortal language and a heavenly harmony with which to bring it all to a grand and glorious finale.*

Unexpected joy

Edward and Rachel had always longed to return to Nigeria, if for only a visit. That hope slipped away along with her health. Following her death, it never entered his mind again until questions were posed that made his eyes brighten. Stinson and his family were going to Ogbomosho, Nigeria on a medical mission trip and for the inauguration of the Edward and Rachel Humphrey Nigerian Endowment Fund, a fund set up to honor their service in Nigeria. Would he come along? Would he stay on after they left to teach at the seminary for one semester? The questions hardly needed to be asked. His only regret was that she would not be with him but he knew she was with him in spirit and knew she would want him to go. For him, it would bring closure to a life of service, closure to his ministry and closure to what was his life-long divine calling.

Preparations for the trip began immediately and soon Edward was on a sentimental journey to a land he loved but thought he would never see again. It was the land which had been home to him and his young family over a quarter of a century before. This time, he accompanied Stinson and his family to Nigeria. His return was emotional for Rachel was not with him physically, but he was overjoyed in having Stinson, Arvie and especially his grandchildren share in the experience. He was mindful of a full range of emotions. Capturing these emotions, he wrote: "not only are there reminders on every hand of the dear days of long ago and of the young family who were then my pride and joy; there were also stark reminders of the brevity of our human existence, the frail character of our finitude, and the expendability of one's particular contribution in Kingdom service."

Stinson and his family stayed in Nigeria less than two weeks, enjoying every precious moment of time with their father and grandfather as he explored the place he called home so many years before. Edward stayed on to teach at the Nigerian Baptist Theological Seminary for the fall semester of 1993. He relished the opportunity to be where he had experienced some of the most rewarding years of his life and welcomed the chance to, once again, influence the lives of young Nigerian seminary students.

The journey back to Nigeria was also a memorable one. In letters to family back home, Edward told of renewed friendships from years gone by, including those with Joseph Ilori and Morakinyo Taiwo, both orphans and former students who became members of the family. At a pastor's conference, he talked with Mr. John Lawale, one of the teachers who served with him at the Teacher Training College in Ede in 1949 as well as another teacher from his initial days at Iwo in 1948. New acquaintances with a new generation of missionaries gave him encouragement. The progress in Christian witness and visits to large churches he once knew to be small and struggling moved him deeply.

In a tribute to Rachel on the first anniversary of her death, Edward held a memorial service in the land they loved and once called home. It was a service he wanted to have and one he felt he needed to have. It too brought closure to the ministry that was theirs as *one*. The memorial service brought together the current missionaries in

Ogbomosho and Edward's very special friends who had also come to teach for a semester at the seminary as the first recipients of the Humphrey Nigerian Endowment Fund. Jerry and Joanne Stubblefield were at the seminary during the same semester Edward was there and played a meaningful role in the service remembering Rachel.

Near the beginning of the semester, Edward was asked to speak in chapel. The last time he spoke in chapel at the seminary in Nigeria had been about a week before the family had frantically left Nigeria because of Rachel's illness. On that occasion in 1965, he was unaware that he would be leaving Nigeria so soon, his missionary career at an end. The subject he chose to use in chapel that day so long ago he called, "The Form of a Servant." Throughout the intervening years, he had often thought of that final message in chapel and wondered what he would say if given the chance to speak again, the chance to say "one word more." Given that chance, he chose the same title again, but the content of his message had radically changed to accommodate his yearning for "one word more." In Edward's message, "... (he) presumed to assess something of the meaning and the mystery of the divine self-emptying whereby the very Lord of glory assumed in 'inexpressible' love 'the form of a servant.' If ever there was a theme so lofty and so far exceeding the range of human comprehension as to utterly deplete the resources of the searching mind, it is surely that of 'the love of Christ.'"

Leaving Nigeria

As happened in 1965, when Edward began to prepare to leave Nigeria to return home, visitors began to come for one last visit, to pay their respects and say good-bye. He joyously received the loving farewell visits of those whose lives he touched and of those who touched his. Of the latter, were many he was unable to see when hurriedly leaving in 1965. For days, they steadily came to express their love in the Nigerian way that never really says good-bye but means "until we meet again." This time there was time to linger, to visit, to share and to reminisce before he departed.

In a final message to the faculty and student body during a farewell chapel service, Edward's message entitled "One Word More" spoke about the biblical Rachel, his own Rachel and a life of shared ministry. It was a message from his heart and as he so often said before, "In matters of the heart, there must always be the felt need for 'one word more.'"

Edward with Dr. Obaje, President of Nigerian Baptist Theological Seminary, Ogbomosho (seminary in background), 1993

Edward with his Nigerian seminary students in 1993

Travis Collins, a missionary in Nigeria at the time, gave a tribute to Edward for the occasion. Speaking on behalf of the faculty and students, he noted Edward had reminded those at the seminary of many things:

"...of the importance of thinking...of the call to mission...of our children...of our spouses and our vows...of journeying on past the crises of our lives." And "for four short months"... "(we) were in the presence of one who walks closely with God."

This time, Edward left on his own terms. There was no mad dash to Lagos to catch a plane, no fear of the unknown and no sense of impending doom. He left grateful for the time God had once again given him to serve in the land of his childhood dreams. This time he left in peace, his heart filled with joy and gratefully aware of the goodness and love of God.

As the day of departure drew near, one final demonstration of kindness and love remained in Edward's heart. The student dormitories were quiet that Sunday afternoon as he visited each of his students one by one to bid each a fond farewell. Determined to leave with one final act of kindness and love as was so graciously shown to him that sad day in 1965, he paused at each student's room where he lingered to offer words of encouragement, kindness, appreciation and love. As he moved on to speak with another, the others began to gather in small groups. They watched silently. They watched lovingly. They watched in awe, aware of the presence of God.

Leaving Nigeria for a final time, Edward felt rewarded by the experience and encouraged by what he had witnessed. The few months there, he said, "provided something of a capstone for my life and service in this world." They brought to him a most satisfying sense of closure to what he regarded as almost a life-long sense of divine calling. He flew back to California to the open arms of a proud and loving family. This time he experienced much joy but time would be required to appreciate the goodness of God in giving him the opportunity to return to a place so dear to his heart. This time he had completed his mission; his joy knew no bounds! Grateful to God, he said, "Whatever else remains to me, this will be the crowning event of it all."

Home sweet home

Upon his return, Edward set about the happy task of catching up with friends and family. His heart was filled with warm memories that he wanted to share. Over several weeks, he visited each of his children and their families, reliving his experiences and catching up with their lives. He had visited places his children remembered, places where they had spent their childhood. A warm glow settled over him as he shared and relived the memories of old and new friends, places of his dearest of memories and times of a happy past. He wanted his grandchildren to understand his love for Africa and his sense of calling to missions. He felt a duty to impart his call of service to them, and he wanted them to know and understand more fully the nature of their grandmother and the ministry they shared through a life together. Above all else, he wanted them to know and love God.

Turning to his study, Edward began to write. Although he would never complete what he set out to write, his intention was to cover topics he wished to leave as a kind of blueprint for his walk with God. It was his way of leaving a written account of his own legacy, a way to hand down to his grandchildren a portion of their heritage that they might know and understand his darling, their love, their ministry and their love of God. His fervent desire was for his grandchildren to know as much as he could impart about their grandmother but more importantly, he wanted them to know and understand their faith and their walk with God. His hope for their lives was that they too would know the joy and fulfillment of an intimate knowledge and love of God. And so he wrote of faith, Christian faith, his greatest source of strength and courage. He wrote of his own experiences of mortal love and the reality of divine love. He wrote of the mysterious nature of death and the reality of eternal life that lies beyond what he called the "impenetrable veil of death." He wrote of hope, the hope gained from an intimate knowledge of God, his walk with God, his hope for his grandchildren.

Foregleam of eternal life

In the summer of 1999, Edward developed shortness of breath. Only when he could no longer take his usual long, leisurely walks around his neighborhood did he casually mention it to his son. The fact that he had even mentioned it was of great concern to Stinson for his father had ignored symptoms of serious illness before. There was the episode just before retirement that eventually led to coronary artery bypass surgery. Several months before Rachel's death, Edward had one day casually mentioned to Stinson that he was having trouble using his right arm. At that time, he suffered a very mild stroke but recovered quickly and completely without hospitalization.

His shortness of breath led to a radiograph that revealed the buildup of fluid within his right chest cavity, on his right lung. Once the fluid was removed, his breathing briefly returned to normal but a pathology report on the fluid that was removed provided the definitive diagnosis—adenocarcinoma of the lung, a fast growing cancer that was already inoperable and had spread throughout his lungs. Edward remained hospitalized for a few days after the fluid was removed for further testing and to begin addressing some of the issues he faced with an aggressive terminal illness. These included, among others, proper diet, pain control, hospice, contact with a social worker and the likely need for a caregiver as well as a discussion of the expectations for the course of his disease. His outlook was realistic for throughout life there were many times he had faced trial, hardship and adversity. Now as before, there was no bitterness, no anger, no questioning, no resentment nor grief. He faced his cancer the way he had faced life, with implicit trust in God. His faith provided certain peace; his eternal hope sustained him.

Edward wanted to make an informed decision regarding treatment of the cancer. As usual, he sought to learn all he could about possible alternatives of treatment and sought an honest appraisal of the prognosis. With so much information to absorb, he asked Stinson to accompany him on his visits with each of the specialists involved with his case. Each time the discussions were unhurried, calm, thoughtful and kind. The oncologist confirmed what he already knew in his heart. The doctor was kind and gentle but spoke in a forthright manner that Edward appreciated. The widespread nature of the cancer precluded any realistic hope that chemotherapy or radiation would improve quality of life or measurably prolong his life. Calmly accepting what he heard, he drew strength from his unwavering relationship with God and felt a sense of contentment and peace of mind, realizing in his own temporal passage a "foregleam of the eternal."

To God be the glory

Hospice became immediately involved with the many and varied end-of-life issues that arise in such situations. Edward became particularly attached to Denise, the nurse assigned by hospice to his case, as did she to him. Their relationship became mutually beneficial.

Each grew fond of the other, looked forward to their visits and Edward particularly enjoyed telling her about Rachel and their story of love. Denise often commented on Edward's faith and trust in God. She would linger to talk about God, attempting to gain insight into Edward's own spirituality. She openly claimed to glean a greater understanding of her own spirituality from her discussions with him.

As the months of summer waned, so did Edward's level of energy. It very rapidly became apparent that he required a caregiver of his own. Through the social worker assigned to him while he was hospitalized, the family was placed in contact with a service that provided caregivers for patients requiring all levels of care. Interviews took place but from their initial meeting, Edward and Jim seemed like long-time friends. Jim had acted as a caregiver for several years with many patients and had a record of loyalty to the patients entrusted to his care. Initially hired to work only a few days a week, Jim became attached to Edward and soon lived at Edward's home, taking off only one or two days a week. He remained loyal to Edward until the end.

Edward and Jim's lives met and crossed with little in common yet conversation, trust and enjoyment of one another's companionship came easily. Jim was an affable character but it was readily apparent to Edward that there was a certain emptiness in his life. Jim marveled at Edward's peace of mind as he faced a terminal disease, but he provided exactly what Edward needed. There existed a vast difference in background, education, and outlook yet they joked, loved the same music and at Edward's insistence, had a devotional time each evening. Uncomfortable initially, Jim soon came to look forward to their time of Bible reading and prayer. During the months that followed, Jim learned during these devotions what Edward meant when he often said that he lived "to glorify God in wonder, love and praise." Edward guided Jim as he learned to pray and during the final weeks of his life, Edward nurtured him as he began his walk with God. Edward's patience with Jim's spiritual immaturity was a testament to his own humility as well as his love for those from all walks of life. Jim's patience with Edward's thorough, detailed discussions of theology was testament to the respect and love he had for Edward as well as his own heartfelt yearning to know God. Each felt the goodness, love and blessing offered by the other.

Eventide

A steady stream of family, friends, former students, and fellow church members came with friendship, kindness and love to fill Edward's days with joy as the time of his earthly existence grew short. Each left filled with the peace, love and hope of one steadfast in faith to the end. Each of his grandchildren came with words of love just as Edward had done long before with his own grandfather, Neill.

Stinson's visits with his father during his last days were spent in quiet and loving conversation. They both knew the end was near. With each breath, he labored as he struggled to say each word. As he had many times before, he spoke of his deep love for words and the ideas that words were able to express. He had thought much about the mystery of death, and in his usual eloquent way, expressed a desire to "say his last words with meaningful dignity and profundity." During one of their last visits together, he held out his hand to hold Stinson's hand and asked that they pray together. Gasping with great difficulty between strenuous breaths, Edward prayed aloud, "O Lord, I present myself unto Thee. I come into your presence at your mercy. Amen." Words from a poem Edward had written several years earlier entitled "An Evening Reverie" rang ever true:

O divine love, ever changing
Essence of divine Being.
What grace is hereby given to Thy
Creatures before Thee kneeling.

O divine Peace, dear gift of Thy love,
Blest balm for the weary soul.
How tranquil our dear refuge in Thee
When we by grace are made whole.

Morning glory

As the early hours of Sunday, December 12, 1999 approached, Edward found each breath as painful as it was strenuous. Yet he was at peace, eager to resume with Rachel the glorious strains of a symphony of love and above all, yearning to look upon the face of God.

During his final hours of earthly life, prayer and exchanges of love and appreciation with each of his children brought comfort and distraction from the discomfort and difficulty with breathing. Then, suddenly, as if enraptured by the loveliest of voices, he looked heavenward, summoned Home to the melodic strains of a heavenly symphony. In the glory of the early morning, the grandeur of an unfinished symphony once again played the music of love as he was reunited with his "darling." Edward was now in the presence of God, the One he loved above all else and had served so well as a good and faithful servant.

Remembering

"In the words of the Ecclesiast, 'the silver cord... (is now) loosed; the golden bowl ... (is) broken; the pitcher... (is) broken at the fountain; the dust (has returned) to the earth as it was; and the spirit (has returned) unto God who gave it.'" These were words Edward used to notify friends and loved ones of Rachel's transition to her heavenly home, words that now seemed appropriate for his own. For his entire life, Edward attempted to live in a responsible manner before God. As a Christian, he based his life on four central virtuous themes: truth, faith, love and hope. As he faced death, he did so with profound dignity, grace and peace.

Edward was remembered foremost for his commitment to God, his service of Him and his faith in Him. His devotion to Rachel was intertwined with their call to a life of ministry and service to God. He lived the life envisioned by Rachel's promise to him on the inscription she placed within his wedding band, "All That I Am." As a husband, he was that bulwark of strength, tenderness and character that brought joy and satisfaction to her heart. As a father, he was an example of strength, kindness, tenderness and grace to his children in a way that engendered their desire to emulate his own life. As a grandfather, he demonstrated an unselfish love that allowed his grandchildren to know the meaning of marriage as an act of resolute hope in which each believes in the other and both see the purpose of God written upon the whole of life. To some he was remembered as "a true saint," others thought of him lovingly as "Saint Edward" and to still others "as nearly a perfect a man as ever existed." To all, he was a respected friend, an example of faith, gentleness, humility and optimism in the face of unimaginable adversity. His life was a joyful example of walking in truth and faith with God. With a total lack of remonstration and with an unusual presence of peace, he endured a long and painful terminal illness. To the end, he was an example to all in his presence of how to die with faith, dignity, peace and confidence.

The day after he died, a small piece of paper was discovered on his bedside table on which he had feebly written, "Death is without exception the greatest mystery of mortal existence. It marks the cessation of a stream of human consciousness." Through the mercy of God, he retained his unusual ability to speak with dignity, clarity, and eloquence until the end of his life. Now in the presence of God, he spoke with the "immortal language" of love and praise.

AN EVENING REVERIE

O divine Truth, resplendent in the
Radiance of Thy glory.
How the Mystery of life is gilt
With the joy of Thy story.

O divine Love, ever unchanging
Essence of divine Being.
What grace is hereby given to Thy
Creatures before Thee kneeling.

O divine Peace, dear gift of Thy love,
Blest balm for the weary soul.
How tranquil our dear refuge in Thee
When we by grace are made whole.

O divine Hope, unfailing shield in
Sorrow, death, or dark despair.
How wondrous sweet when day is done to
Find retreat in Thy Repair.

J. Edward Humphrey
At eventide

An Evening Reverie

A MORNING REVEILLE

When morning breaks and shadows flee,
A glad new day is dawning.
With grateful hearts and new resolve
We lift our praise, dear Lord, to Thee.

Through the long watches of the night,
Sweet rest and peace Thou gavest.
No ill beguiled Thy watchful eye,
No darkness hid from us Thy light.

Go Thou before us now this day;
Make plain the path Thou choosest.
In joy or sorrow, peace or pain,
We gladly follow in Thy way.

From morn to eve, be Thou our Guide;
Break to us "the Bread of life."
Lead to "springs of living water."
And little would be ask beside.

Save, that when our days are ended,
We may dwell at Home with Thee,
Where the gates are ajar by day,
And night forever suspended.

J. Edward Humphrey
At blush of dawn

A Morning Reveille

The Music Plays On

Human love is what it is first of all before God and unto God, and therefore it is primarily the response of obedience to its Lord.

Edward and Rachel's relationship throughout earthly life was first a relationship based on their profound faith in God, His will, and His purpose for their lives. Only in terms of their faith, can one think of the magnitude of their love and devotion for one another. Their faith gave them the strength to endure the circumstances they faced throughout life. Believing that each was "all that I am" to the other sustained them and gave them the confidence to carry out their ministry.

For over forty-five years, Edward and Rachel shared life together at the deepest level of human emotion. Living as *one*, their love was a nearly perfect blending of the spiritual and physical qualities of love through marriage before God. Their explicit trust and faith in God throughout the ordeal they endured became their final ministry to countless others. Devotion to God was consistent throughout their lives. Devotion to one another in the presence of unimaginable adversity was an inspiration to those who knew them. Their lives continue to be a blessing to their children and grandchildren, who honor and adore their memory.

Expressions of love

In the months leading up to their wedding in 1947, Edward and Rachel each found a unique and eloquent way to express their love one to the other. Rachel's Christmas gift to Edward in 1946 was a copy of *Sonnets From The Portuguese* by Elizabeth Barrett Browning. Inside the front cover, she wrote an expressive note of her love for him.

SONNETS
FROM THE PORTUGUESE
Elizabeth Barrett Browning

Written upon the pages
of this book you will find
my love for you expressed
in a way I am not able
to express it.

I hope you will enjoy
it -- not only during this
Christmas season but always.

Darling, I love you
deeply - You are all I want
in any one person and I
say with all the sincerity
of my soul these simple
but expressive words - I love
you!

All my love always
Rachel

Note from Rachel to Edward inside front cover of
Sonnets From The Portuguese, 1946

211

Rachel included a typed copy of sonnet #43, a poem entitled "How Do I Love Thee?" and inserted it within the front cover of the book, which reads,

> *How do I love thee? Let me count the ways.*
> *I love thee to the depth and breadth and height*
> *My soul can reach, when feeling out of sight*
> *For the ends of being and ideal grace.*
> *I love thee to the level of every day's*
> *Most quiet need, by sun and candle-light.*
> *I love thee freely, as men strive for right.*
> *I love thee purely, as they turn from praise.*
> *I love thee with the passion put to use*
> *In my old griefs, and with my childhood's faith.*
> *I love thee with a love I seemed to lose*
> *With my lost saints. I love thee with the breath,*
> *Smiles, tears, of all my life; and, if God choose,*
> *I shall but love thee better after death.*

On the back of the small piece of paper on which she had typed the poem, she inscribed,

This poem expresses the way I feel about thee and I love with all my heart. I love you sincerely Edward and as the days and weeks go by I will love thee more if it is God's will.

With all my love,
Rachel

On the Easter before they were married in May 1947, Edward, in a tender expression of his love for Rachel wrote what would serve as a prelude to the way he would forever think of her, writing,

> My Darling,   Easter Eve
>
> I passed far deep into the garden of love today, and paused at each turn of the way to re-live the moments which hallow those sacred spots to me. As I wandered I plucked a blossom here and there with which to adorn the Queen of My Heart.
>
> Your,
> Edward

Edward and Rachel began their walk through life together as *one* with an uncommon understanding of love, its selfless nature, and an enduring commitment to one another. During the years that followed, they grew closer to one another and to God. He was the stabilizing force in their lives, the One whose plan for their lives they patiently waited to follow at every turn.

The "Other Victims"

Asked to contribute to a proposed book to be published under the title *The Other Victims,* Edward, instead wrote what he termed "a positive affirmation ...of the personhood and the needs of 'a significant other.'" He was not able to accept the concept that he was in some way "the other victim," for he viewed the care and support of Rachel as the highest privilege in the world. From his point of view, Rachel had set the tone for their marriage when she had inscribed within his wedding band the words, "All That I Am." Her words, he wrote, were "simple, eloquent, and unconditional" words that over the "ensuing years ...

disclosed how utterly genuine and unreserved ... that commitment had been."

When they left Nigeria, Rachel had openly expressed anguished dismay at causing the one she loved to leave the place and work he had dreamed of since adolescence, the ministry to which they had been called. But the memory of their marriage vows and what Edward said was "the matchless expression of self-giving engraved in (his) ring" caused him to tell her, "You are my darling! Whatever happens to one of us happens to both of us. We will face this thing together. And whatever happens to you, as long as God gives me strength, I will be there. I will be there for you with 'all that I am.'"

For the remainder of Rachel's life, a particularly progressive and virulent form of multiple sclerosis caused an almost inconceivable range of physical disabilities. They both accepted her illness with grace, propriety and a beautiful spirit. They maintained a loving disposition that was both extraordinary and uncommon and faced their circumstances with a shared Christian faith. In the reality of divine love, they found sustaining assurance and peace of mind and heart.

Edward was well aware that "it might very well have been (him) rather than her who was stricken" with a life-altering disease. He had no doubt if that had been the case, "she would have been there for (him) with untiring devotion and with the most tender love to attend (his) needs." It was therefore a proposition he could not accept that he was in some way "the other victim."

A love story[18]

Edward and Rachel found in each other that for which their hearts were restless. In her, Edward had found the ideal of purity, grace, and sweetness, which had been the substance of his highest and holiest dreams. In him, Rachel had found strength, tenderness, and character, which brought joy and satisfaction to her heart. By the mercy of God, their separate wanderings ceased, and through the vows of marriage, they performed an act of unveiled love, engaging in an utter act of faith and entering a solemn covenant as comprehensive as life itself. Because they believed in one another to the very end with resolute hope, they sought the purpose of God at every point in their lives,

---

[18]   Adapted from wedding ceremony Edward composed for and used by his children and grandchildren

and with the help of God, they sustained and nurtured all they found true and good in one another. As completely as they knew how and were able, they shared the whole of life. In sickness and in health, in adversity and prosperity, sustained by faith, they demonstrated a love as true and hopeful as the poetic words describing love found in I Corinthians, 13: 4–7:[19]

Love is very patient, very kind,
Love knows no jealousy;
Love makes no parade, gives itself no airs,
Is never rude, never selfish, never irritated, never resentful;
Love is never glad when others go wrong,
Love is gladdened by goodness, always slow to expose,
Always eager to believe the best,
Always hopeful, always patient.
Love never disappears.

All that I am

Edward and Rachel fully embraced the inscription she placed within his wedding ring, "All That I Am," as a way of life with each other, in their ministry and, above all, before God. Through divine love and their togetherness as *one*, they found enduring peace as they overcame the complexities of severe illness, life, and even death itself. Through profound faith, the security of their trust in God and the acceptance of His plan for their lives, they came to a complete understanding of their own togetherness and interconnectivity of living as *one*. Their love traverses all boundaries of time and has no end. It is a love that plays as a symphony, a symphony never finished in mortal life but one that plays on in eternal life. The melodies of that symphony continue to play in the celestial garden of love accompanied by the harmonious voices of a heavenly host of angels through all of eternity.

Through faith, love and life are eternal.

---

[19]   James Moffat translation

Afterword

by Susan Perkins and Edna Rachel Miller

Edna Rachel: When I first heard about a book about our parents' lives and love, my first reaction was "it will be nice to have their story in print." However, the more I thought about it, the more excited I became to see the finished product for I feel incredibly blessed to have been born to my parents. They were and are such an inspiration to me, the way I approach life, and my own marriage and relationships. The example they provided was the best when it came to being a servant, and the love they shared was more than special, it was incredible.

The first question that came as my brother began collecting information was, "What do you think an appropriate title would be for their story?" My first thought and both my brother and sister agreed, was it could only be "All That I Am," the inscription within my father's wedding band. It epitomized their relationship and became the inscription on my mother's headstone after she died. Their lives together were truly about giving all of themselves both to each other and to God's purpose. In this book, we now have a written accounting of our parents, two soul mates who profoundly touched everyone with whom they came in contact.

Susan: Our parents met in college and fell in love as college students, both pursuing the best education they could get to meet the high requirements demanded of missionaries appointed at that time. However, this was not a lack-luster, practical, or sensible arrangement suitable for two people whose career paths were merging. This was a dizzy falling in love, when the air is perfumed, the whole world is beautiful, sunlight and moonlight were made just for lovers, when all of creation sings a love song! They could never speak of it without their faces lighting up at the sweet remembrance of it. My father was not able to concentrate in class. They both chafed under the watchful eye of the women's dorm mother, and took long walks just to be alone, to read love poems to each other and to have private conversation. Finally, the great day came when the ring was paid for, the breathless proposal made and accepted, and two hearts came together as one with their first kiss under the blazing glory of trees on fire with fall foliage in the golden rays of late afternoon sun. Theirs was a love filled with uncontainable gladness, made even more wondrous by the joyful realization that their finding of one another had been part of God's plan all along. The Divine Matchmaker had given them as a special gift to each other, even though each had been willing to go to Africa alone if necessary. They had not only a calling to share God's love with the world, but also a calling to a pure, self-giving, unreserved and unconditional love for each other that would be a declaration to the world of the passionate love of the Creator for the people of His own beloved creation. They never said it that way, of course. They just lived it, day in and day out, with shared rejoicing in times of happiness and shared comfort in times of grief and debilitation, always receiving, as from the Lord's hand, the myriad blessings and unfathomable sorrow that are part of human existence this side of heaven. They faced the unknown together, sailing off to African soil with the certainty of God's presence with them, leaving family and everything familiar behind them, content to follow the footsteps of Jesus wherever they night lead.

Edna Rachel: It was not until I became an adult that I realized the risks they had taken in their lives. Growing up in Nigeria was such a natural part of our lives that I had taken it for granted. It was after a conversation with my father about my own marriage plans that I realized the steps of faith they took. He was concerned because I was considering a life with a man of twenty-nine who had aspirations of going to the University of Jerusalem to study. The similarities of our relationship and theirs came into clear vision at that point for he was twenty-nine at the time he and my mother were married and they went to Africa shortly thereafter. Travel plans with my future husband, Sandy, did not come to fruition but that conversation was an important revelation in a father-daughter relationship. When I think of them, setting foot aboard ship for that first voyage to Nigeria, married for about a year, I am amazed at their willingness to freely go and serve God in a foreign land. In more modern times, we feel a need to have everything in order before we can proceed with any plans, but they were willing to go into the unknown, have and raise their children, and become a family in a strange land, all because God said "Go". They went in faith, not only in their God, but also in each other.

Susan: Our parents were happy in their adopted homeland. There was never a martyr complex or groaning about hardship. They reared their children in a land of venomous snakes and parasites. My sister and I constantly had open sores on our arms and legs from scratching insect bites. It was several years before we had electricity, and that was for only four hours a day. There was no drinkable water, so rain water had to be caught and filtered. There were no local stores, only the open air market. The slightest necessity took planning and foresight. Yet, we had many friends among the African people and the mission family. We felt safe. We were at home. My mother would always take time during the day to play with us, games of Rook on the front porch or croquet in the yard. Daddy built us a tree house (really a platform with a ladder) so we could climb up and swing out on a chain. Mother made homemade doughnuts and snicker doodle cookies and brought them to us and our friends at boarding school. She made angel food birthday cakes, even one with a doll standing in the middle-the cake being the doll's skirt. I would fall asleep at night listening to the talking drums in surrounding villages, and the low hum of my parents' voices talking over the day.

Our parents had their assigned duties as missionaries but they never knew what the day might bring. People with large open sores would come to our door for medicine. Mother would wash, medicate and dress these wounds as a matter of course. Our father would sometimes be called out to transport a laboring mother (a Madonna and child, as he put it) from one of the villages to the hospital. Our parents were always in a giving mode, responding to the needs around them. I would say they had a servant heart, but they did not really think about it that way. They were always on the same page, in harmony, sharing their call and their service. Mother sometimes talked about how the Foreign Mission Board had tried to prepare new missionaries for "culture shock," but they never found anything shocking. They loved what they did, and found contentment and fulfillment in it.

I do not remember any arguing between my parents. Although there were occasional miscommunications, we grew up in a peaceful home. Daddy was the gracious, dignified professor. Mother blurted out whatever crossed her mind. Daddy was constantly mindful of implications or innuendo of what he said or worried whether people would be offended by it. Mother was just herself, more direct and not afraid to express her feelings. They balanced each other and tempered each other, but never tried to change each other.

Daddy was the deep thinker and Mother was the practical one who got on with whatever life presented. This was the way they both reacted to the long years of coping with multiple sclerosis. The implications of Mother's progressive debilitation reverberated in the depths of Daddy's soul. He was constantly thinking of ways to make her life easier. Mother always seemed unfazed by it. I remember once that as a young nurse fresh out of nursing school, I asked Mother how she coped with her illness. She said, "I just don't think about it." That answer did not fit with the classes I had had on psychological reactions to illness, and I was convinced that she was in a hardened state of denial. However, over the years, I came to realize that she had told the truth. Mother was a realist to the core, but she did not dwell on her illness. She was determined that multiple sclerosis was not who she was. I came to appreciate how much easier she made this experience for the rest of her family by being herself and getting on with life. Just as they had faced the unknown together in Africa, so they faced an unknown future with multiple sclerosis—together, with an unfaltering faith in the goodness and sovereignty of God. If God allowed it, then they would trust Him to fulfill His purposes through it. From the first night of their marriage, they had adopted the matchless words of Romans 8 to be their special message from God, their pillar of strength to cling to through whatever life would hold for them. "All things work together for good for those who love God, who are called according to His purpose...", and "nothing in all creation will be able to separate us from the love of God in Christ Jesus our Lord."

Edna Rachel: Mother and Daddy's love story became even more precious with the onset of Mother's illness. In my nursing career, I have been witness to families suddenly facing life-altering conditions. Some have faced it better than others have. Mother and Daddy epitomized the marriage vow to love "in sickness or in health". We live in a society that promises to love each other until it gets too hard, but I feel so fortunate to have witnessed my parents, not only staying together through tough times, but thriving on their love for one another during those times as well. In spite of her handicaps, Mother would try to keep some normalcy in their home while Daddy spent long hours at the seminary. Among my favorite memories is of Mother playing her favorite game, Scrabble, or the card game, Rook with us. I remember Mother silently laughing during some of those games. She always wished she could laugh aloud but instead you would just see her shoulders shaking and her face becoming flushed as she laughed. It was not long before we were all enveloped in giggles. I loved being witness to the tenderness that Daddy showed to Mother. He would call her his "sweetie". Not a day went by without him telling her that he loved her.

The example set by both of our parents is undeniable. They had a selfless giving spirit, and demonstrated their love to each other, their three children, and to just about everyone they met. If they were able to meet a need that presented itself to them, they would cheerfully do just that. I still remember my first trip home from college. I did not have a car so I decided to take the Greyhound bus home. It was an interesting trip; fraught with being accosted at the bus station and learning to deal with groups of people far different from that I was accustomed to. Once Daddy heard of the adventure, he simply said, "any time you want to come home, just call me and I will come and get you." Looking back, those trips were so special. It was just the two of us. I do not remember the details of any profound conversation, just the usual discussions about school and plans but with a father who listened intently, was interested and openly loved me. I remember how special it was to have his undivided attention for the hour and a half drive.

One of the most wonderful parts of their story in my mind was God's provision for them. They were so faithful to His purposes and He provided for them in all things. They were never wealthy but the richness of their lives was evident. They never owned a home, but one was always available to them. When their missionary career ended, God opened the doors at Golden Gate Seminary for them. Even as health became a large issue for them, God had seen fit to lead all three of their children into the medical field, which gave them medical resources to help meet their needs. God is good and it inspires me to see how our parents lived their lives in faith that He would supply all their needs. It reminds me that He knows my every need before I even ask Him and will supply my every need.

I am grateful that both of my children were able to know their grandparents. Grandpa Humphrey came to stay with them over a weekend get-away that I took with my husband. Every now and then, I still hear, with amusement, about things that happened over those two days. My son, Joshua, likes to tell about the time that Otis, our seventy-five pound German shorthaired pointer, pushed past Grandpa and was running across our front yard towards an elderly man who was walking down the street. Otis was very people friendly but Grandpa did not know that. It was the only time Joshua heard Grandpa issue a stern command to Otis. He said Otis stopped dead in his tracks and dutifully came back. From then on, Otis had a newfound respect for Grandpa, and never left his side the rest of the weekend. Although Joshua and my daughter, Elizabeth, were still young when their grandparents died, they remember their character and I hope will remember their gentle, loving spirit that set them apart.

Susan: Over the years I watched Daddy become Mother's hands and feet, lending her the strength of his muscles, holding back the relentless debilitation as long as possible, fighting for her life as though it was his own. When he had a stroke causing weakness on one side of his body, he did not call for help most of the day, but continued taking care of her. I came to care for both of them during this time and had to restrain him from trying to care for her with one arm. She was his beloved Rachel, and she needed him. Over the years, I drove the hundred miles to visit and help out many times, yet even with years of nursing experience I could never care for Mother the way Daddy did. They were one heart, one soul and one mind, and his touch was like no other.

A few days before Mother died, I was preparing to leave to return home after a visit, and about to say my good-byes. Mother held me with her gaze with eyes full of such love and tenderness and warmth, that I was drawn over to her chair, and found myself saying "I love you too." She had not been able to speak for some time, and had no way of getting my attention other than for me to notice the intensity of the way she looked at me. It was our last communication. The next time I saw her she was comatose. The night before she died Daddy pulled up a recliner chair next to her bed to watch over her. I saw him in the soft lamplight standing next to her, gazing down at her with his hands folded, praying. His posture was so humble, so submissive. The fight was over. She was beyond his reach. He had accompanied her all the way to the gates and was handing her over to the only One who loved her more than he did.

Daddy never took off his wedding ring. The love between my parents was an indisputable fact and has been a defining and stabilizing force for me all my life. It became for me the standard and very definition of true love. Anything less is a shallow imitation. Love "bears all things, believes all things, hopes all things, endures all things. Love never ends."

Appendix A
Anniversary letters

On our fifth wedding anniversary

May 23, 1952

My Darling Rachel,

These five years have brought a world of sweetness into my life. The confidence and trust which you continually inspire within me becomes more sacred with the passing years. Your ideal, ever present sweetheart love burns its way ever more deeply into my very being, and thereby awakens a charm and wonder too deep-seated for utterance. Your steadfast loyalty to our avowed purpose of service in bringing to a lost world the glorious Gospel of the Son of Righteousness continues to be a joy to me. And Darling, we are so dependent upon each other's faithfulness at that point!

In the blessed experience of parenthood you have been the ideal mother to our children, proving yourself completely worthy of the name.

I thank God for you, Rachel, and pray that I may prove in some measure worthy of your love.

All of my love always,
Edward

On our twenty-fifth wedding anniversary

May 23, 1972

My Darling,

Every tender emotion of the heart and all the joys of living are mingled in every thought of you. These twenty-five years have laid bare before my eyes how profoundly and unreservedly you spoke that day when you uttered those beautiful, frightening words-"All that I am."

As cherished companion of my life you have enriched every aspect of my being immeasurably by submerging your own. You have been all and more than I could ever have dreamed when we began our happy pilgrimage together. I have long been poignantly aware that many of the opportunities, educational and otherwise, which have brought enrichment to my own life were afforded only through your selfless devotion, ever given without the slightest hint that you were aware of the cost to yourself.

And I shall never be able to reveal to you the full measure of my over-flowing gratitude that you have been the wonderful mother you have to our children. Again, you have submerged your own life for the sake of theirs. The abiding ideals of Christian character and purpose which we observe with unceasing joy in each of them is more than anything else the fruit of blessed motherhood.

You faithful devotion in mission service and your continuing encouragement in all that God has given me to be and to do have been to this day the supreme human source of my strength. Whether in the delivery of a sermon, the preparation of a lesson, the experience of prayer, or in just plain living, I am the stronger, the purer, the more satisfied when you are there. With all my heart, I thank my God for you.

And Darling, I love you for the brave, cheerful, uncomplaining manner with which you have borne your present illness. God is surely working in His mysterious way for good and for His own glory. I am persuaded that there is some glorious, hidden purpose in all of this which shall yet be revealed and that far beyond your present sufferings there is laid up for you a crown of life.

In a manner more profound than I could have understood twenty-five years ago, I say again with all my heart: "...to have and to hold from this day forward...in sickness and in health, to love and to cherish, till death do us part...."

In tenderest love,
Your Edward

On our forty-second wedding anniversary

May 23, 1989

My Darling,

This day finds your devoted husband in a many-sided reflective mood. The sobering circumstances of recent weeks have served to remind us yet again of the fragile character of our earthly existence. But they have also deepened awareness of the blessed meaning of Christian faith and hope. They have added, moreover, a more profound sense of the essence of precious time spent together in soul to soul rapport. We know, of course, that we shall never be able to recapture lost opportunities nor redress even to our own satisfaction past failures. But by the grace of God, it may yet be granted us to discover anew something of the fullness of life day by day. For a little while, perhaps, we may still explore together life's inexhaustible potential for finding and identifying with enduring human values.

In swiftly receding patterns, the luster of the "high road" now lies well behind us; before us looms the twilight zone. Cherished dreams remain unfulfilled; absorbing self-appointed tasks appear now to lie beyond our reach. A world of unanswered questions, of both terrestrial and celestial proportion, still bewilder our limited understanding. The former, happily we may yet engage with such equipment and capacity as are yet at our command. The latter, we can but hold in humble abeyance until faith becomes sight.

Meanwhile, one dominant emotion never comes to rest in my soul, never ceases to agitate for some more adequate form of expression. I love you with all the power of my being. Whether at labor or at leisure, in prosperity or in adversity, in triumph or in defeat, in joy or in sorrow, in sickness or in health—in all the vicissitudes of this life, you are my darling! That old flame which you kindled in my heart so long ago can never be reduced to smoldering embers. I am persuaded that even the final frontier post (however near or far, and however severe it may be) can but unveil a new dimension of its light and warmth.

With all my heart,
Your Edward

Written following Rachel's
life-threatening struggle
with pneumonia in both
lungs during the winter
and spring of 1989.

On our forty-third wedding anniversary

May 23, 1990

My Darling,

If I had the soul of a poet, I would employ winged words and lend emotive cadence to the hidden motions of my heart today. Or better yet, if I had at my command the sublime art of a master composer, I would exhaust the whole register of haunting sound in search of strains adequate to convey what can never really be framed in mere word. And I would thus release these poignant inner stirrings of my being in the fond hope that they might somehow find joyful accord in the responsive vibrations of your own soul. But alas, I am neither a poet nor a composer. That which now agitates my soul, therefore, must be clothed meanwhile in the modest garb of lowly pedestrian language, while remaining closely bound to life as we experience it.

Then come with me, my Darling, for yet another stroll down "memory lane." And let us pause once more for an unhurried moment at each hallowed spot where for us love long ago broke asunder the fettered bonds of time and space, and where one and another of the commonplaces of life were forever transfigured. For though we have lingered there a thousand times before, its promise remains undiminished and its treasure inexhaustible.

It seems fitting that we thus acknowledge today in humble gratitude the course of our journey hitherto-and that we appropriate whatever of human wisdom and value is thus afforded. But at this advanced juncture in our earthly pilgrimage, retrospect must never become the dominating focus of our vision. The direction of our course must be ever onward, for at best the path before us is now severely limited. And sooner or later, it must reveal its inevitable terminus.

Then come with me yet again, my Darling, with vision fixed resolutely upon the foreground of our landscape. And let us together renew our search for fresh vistas on truth and faith and love and hope; and let us venture further in quest of enduring life and godliness. For though foreboding shadows now steal across our path, the dawn of a new and luminous horizon also now beckons us.

With unbounded love and devotion,
Edward

On our forty-fourth wedding anniversary

May 23, 1991

My Darling,

Another anniversary of our happy conjugal union brings unspeakable joy to your devoted husband. For a full forty-and-four wonderful years, you and I have shared life at its deepest human level. And while for one reason or another many of this world's prized attractions have eluded our grasp, we would be the first to acknowledge that in the main, "the lines have fallen" for us "in pleasant places." Ours indeed has been "a goodly heritage" (Psalms 16:6). Through the years, we have been the favored recipients of some of life's choicest gifts and have shared together one of its highest callings.

While it is true that in recent years physical disability has sharply and increasingly restricted the range of our daily orbit and in large measure determined both the options and the character of our separate and our joint endeavors, we do still have each other. And humanly speaking, that fact remains for me at once the supreme joy and the ultimate soul-satisfying reality of our earthly existence. I only long for more wisdom to understand and a greater capacity to appropriate this incomparable blessing while it is still ours to enjoy.

Life moves on for us day by day; yet there is nothing merely ephemeral about it. With each new day, there comes also a wealth of new challenge to explore the meaning, the purpose, and the depths of love. And Darling, I am learning to my ever deepening joy that the story of love is really learned only at long range. It is the prize of a life-long journey through all of the vicissitudes of this life-its variegated succession of events, its ever-changing personal fortunes and conditions, including its trials and disappointments, as well as its gratifying accomplishments and attainments. I am persuaded that only as each burden and disappointment and sorrow, as well as each blessing and victory and joy is mutually and fully shared do we really understand what love is.

All of this, and more, I would now bring into faithful review as I declare once more: "I love you, my Darling, with all my heart and soul." To me, you are a precious gift from God.

Forever yours,
Edward

On our forty-fifth wedding anniversary

May 23, 1992

My Darling,

Today marks the forty-fifth anniversary of our happy rendezvous at the marriage altar. At the human level, the very memory of seeing you approach me there that day remains for me the supreme joy and inspiration of my life. I was literally ecstatic in the realization that you were finally walking into my life, to become inseparably one with me through all of the multi-varied fortunes and alternations of our early existence. And I am still joyfully discovering the boundless range, the fathomless depths, and the matchless beauty of those sacred vows with which we sealed our blessed union. No other human exchange can ever be so precious to me; nor can it be so permanently binding upon "all that I am."

Through all of the intervening years, I have found life with you to be one ever-deepening, uninterrupted story of love-one, moreover, which is uniquely the inviolable property of the heart. It is a story which can never be adequately transcribed from heart to parchment. Mortal language is much too frail for such exalted usage; and mere words, however elegantly chosen, are in this context scarcely more than empty symbols. This is a story which can be communicated only non-verbally from heart to vibrantly responding heart. Yet, it is a story which cannot simply lie dormant in the heart. It is about a love which by its very nature is ever yearning and restless, always and unwaveringly there-and there exclusively for you, my Darling.

Like the well-integrated composition of a majestic symphony with its varied, often complex, and recurring themes, this love is bound-up with all of the components of that life which we have actually experienced together. Whether the focus is upon long-cherished dreams or lost opportunities, perceived achievements or known failures, good health or devastating illness, this love encompasses and embraces them all, believing that even the minor notes which intrude upon our harmony can but lend exquisite and haunting beauty to the whole composition. For after all, the most captivating strains of a great symphony are more often than not the adagio with its subdued, slow-moving sometimes thinly veiled hint of underlying pain or unrelieved sorrow.

Then once more, from deep within the full-orbed circle of our own experience of life together under God, I declare again: "I love you, my Darling, with all my heart and soul."

Forever and ever,
Your Edward

Appendix B
Soliloquies on an Unfinished Symphony

Prelude to Soliloquy on an Unfinished Symphony

May 23, 1993

This is the day (forty-six years removed), and this is the hour (equally far removed) when "my Darling" and I sealed with immortal vows the bonds of our blessed conjugal union. Much indeed remained hidden from our eyes that day as we entered with joy upon the course of our pilgrimage hence. But without exception, all that remained undisclosed at that dear moment has only deepened and beautified the meaning of that exchange. I think that if ever I was in the perfect will of God for my life, I was so at that precious moment. And all of the intervening years have served only to confirm that conviction. To look back upon that expanse of time is to discern the gracious hand of God in all that has transpired. In spite of our own measure of disappointment and heartache, we have believed devoutly with the great Apostle that "in everything God works for good with those who love him, who are called according to his purpose" (Rom. 8:28).

As this particular anniversary has drawn near, I have had to make adjustment in my usual manner of expressing what agitates my soul at this special season. In previous years, I could address my dear one directly as I groped for means of conveying to her what could never find satisfactory embodiment in linguistic form. This year however, I will miss that tangible, total response of her lovely person. At best, this year, I can only recount for myself (and to some extent for my children) the mighty stirrings of my inmost soul as I give myself over to a world of restorative memories. That, I have attempted to do in the content of the accompanying page.

Late this afternoon, I spent a few moments of solitude at her grave-site and remembered! And tonight, my tenderest thoughts turn toward you her family members who remained precious to her until the end.

With my love,
Edward Humphrey

Soliloquy on an Unfinished Symphony #1

On our forty-sixth anniversary
May 23, 1993

For forty-five wonderful years, my darling was always present with me on this "Our Special Day." And with joyful abandon, I could in some measure unveil to her directly (as was my custom) the restless, hidden motions of my heart in her behalf. I never tired of the ceaseless search for more adequate means of conveying to her what in the end would never (and indeed could never!) be framed in frail mortal language, however delicately it might be formulated.

On this forty-sixth anniversary of our blessed union, I find myself once more consciously and painfully alone in the world—alone with a bewildering welter of burdened private thoughts, but more importantly, alone with a priceless store of inviolable memories. As profound as is the depth and range of my solitude, it is mercifully punctuated by a world of precious memories, each of which clamors to be revisited. In this circumstance, our own dear story of life and love is for me continuous. And while henceforth it can only assume the form of a dramatic monologue, that monologue will always be firmly and solely based upon a priceless store of memories accruing from our dear experience of life together.

In the clutches of inescapable solitude, I do find memory to be among the most gracious and sustaining of God's providential gifts. It holds in trust the dearest treasures of the lonely soul. It belongs, moreover, to that inner sanctum of personal being where thieves cannot break through and steal. It is as comprehensive as is life itself, holding each component and the precious content of each single occasion in vivid relief, yet preserving all the while a panoramic vision of the whole. In blessed memory, the very commonplaces of life are all in some sense transposed. And what was in each instance already a thing of joy in its original context, has now in combination become in the Creator's hands a veritable "psalm of angels."

Meanwhile, I confess, the pending lines remain somewhat indistinct (for faith is not yet sight). But faith insists that ultimately, those lines converge at the very throne of grace. Each remembered joy from the dear days of our pilgrimage together, therefore, remains to me an intimation of the perfect fellowship of light in glory.

In loving memory of Rachel, my Darling,
Edward Humphrey, her devoted husband

Soliloquy on an Unfinished Symphony # 2

On our forty-seventh anniversary
May 23, 1994

Ideally, human life is a harmonious composition of many interrelated themes. The very consonance of any particular life lies in the compatibility of the various themes which are woven into its fabric. There are some themes which are potentially as large as life itself and which tend to predominate and to become centers of gravitation for all the others. Some are by nature capable of, and indeed worthy of, wielding great holding power in one's life until one's final hour.

At the human level, incomparably the greatest of these is that conjugal love which was the Creator's first and dearest gift to his highest creatures. With that primordial endowment, mankind became heir of an essence which belongs to heaven itself. For me (through the further gift of precious memory), that pristine bestowment is forever recurrent. In the dear person of Rachel, my Darling, I found (and in the memory of her I still possess in ever deepening intensity) a beauty, a charm, a sweetness, a holy joy which will nourish my soul until mortality "puts on immortality." Day-by-day, and upon every thought of her, a yearning love arises unbidden from the depths of my soul. She brought into my life (and in departing, left to me) a contentment and a sense of human completion which will forever transcend all that is merely temporal. In her companionship, I learned the joy of the union of soul with soul. And in her temporal absence, I am learning the solace of a great hope.

Meanwhile, I would open the windows of my soul to every human exchange wherein faith speaks to Christian faith, and hope speaks to Christian hope. One such word of enduring assurance is proffered with the consummate beauty in a poem by Alfred Tennyson, published in A.D.1850. In his elegy, "In Memoriam," as he slowly worked his way through the pangs of personal grief related to the death of a loved one, he penned these comforting, healing words:

238

"This truth came borne with bier and pall,
I felt it when I sorrowed most,
'Tis better to have loved and lost,
Than never to have loved at all."
And if I may be so irrational as to alter Tennyson's chosen pronouns, I
would borrow a further stanza from his imperishable work of art:
"Forgive my grief for one removed,
Thy creature, whom I found so fair.
I trust [she] lives in thee, and there
I [but] find [her] worthier to be loved."

In loving memory of Rachel, my Darling
Edward Humphrey, her devoted husband

Soliloquy on an Unfinished Symphony #3

On our forty-eighth wedding anniversary
May 23, 1995

In solemn, whispered memory, I wandered alone today through an enchanted garden of love. Down its winding paths I passed unnoticed – paths now overhung by trailing wisps of yesteryear. I ventured far deep into the hallowed precincts of another time and heard once more lingering, haunting echoes from "love's old sweet song": a respite for the weary; a balm for the sad at heart; a curious medley of healing sorrow and divinest joy – a song to be sung in the softly undulating shadows of eventide. With reverent, trembling step and bated breath, I ambled along once familiar lanes and gathered up into my heart the fading vestiges of tracks long since laid in precious company with my Darling. At every turn of the way, my heart released a pent-up sigh, and I left in sacred tithe the tender deposit of a welling, unbidden tear. Here in the caressing arms of healing memory, I was at home once more with the ever-reigning "queen of my heart" – and I was loathe to leave.

In my garden of a love remembered, time itself seemed to stand silent and motionless. Here lay concealed (or at least half concealed) dear treasures of the heart as yet unnamed, for frail mortal language had found no figure of speech with which to clothe those gentle forms. And here, through sweet memory, there still beamed from the lovely countenance of my dear one, indelible, visual accents (more of heaven than of earth) of a story which (in the later months of our sojourn together) had been spoken only through the medium of limpid, glistening eyes, when there was no longer an audible voice to aid in its telling. That which had then been thus spoken from the heart, had been heard in the heart, and there it had been preserved as earth's dearest treasure.

But faith has heard ancient rumor of another garden of love. Its glorious verdure is crowned by "the tree of life," bearing perpetual fruit. The leaves of that tree are reported to be "for the healing of the nations." Through the midst of that garden flows "a river of water of life, clear as crystal, flowing out of the throne of God and of the Lamb." In that dear setting, there will no longer be "anything accursed." And the promise is given that its inhabitants shall look upon the face of God and bear His image upon their foreheads. Through one eternal day (for there is no night there), they shall reign with Him "forever and ever." (Rev. 22:1-5).

And now, free from the physical infirmity which bound her for so long in her earthly life (and divinely cleansed of all human imperfection!), I fancy that my dear one beholds in unhindered, beatific vision the very face of God!

In loving memory of Rachel, my Darling,
Edward Humphrey, her devoted husband

Soliloquy on an Unfinished Symphony #4

On our forty-ninth wedding anniversary
May 23, 1996

On this, our special day, there still lives within my heart a precious finite language human treasure. Beautiful memories and poignant emotions lie dormant there – beyond conceptual or linguistic grasp. A most tender love still waits patiently, yet longingly, to be fashioned and crafted into an expressible form of finite language. Enduring, soul-stirring sentiments never cease to draw sweet harmony from every vivid, personal review of life in company with "my Darling." Together, these private musings of the heart compose a melody that wafts serenely above the din of unfulfilled youthful dreams, above mere fortune and misfortune, above every alternation of mortal pain and sorrow and finite joy. In that blessed harmony, sweet strains of lyrical proportion lend joyful cadence to even the hidden motions of the heart.

For more than forty-five wonderful years, and with the blessing of God, I shared with my dear soul-companion the joys and privileges and responsibilities of temporal conjugal union. At mid-point in our journey together, she fell victim of a virulent, progressive form of the degenerative disease, multiple sclerosis. And for the remainder of her life, under duress, she sought valiantly to present before the world a faithful image of the joy and the goodness of life in the hands of our loving Heavenly Father. But then, just as we were approaching what we are accustomed to regard as "the golden years," she was called away to her eternal home.

To remember my dear one this day must not be to dwell at length, or even primarily, upon the fact or the character of her temporal sufferings. She herself did not appear to do so, even in the most trying episodes of her lengthy ordeal. To the end, she was amazingly patient and cheerful and of sweet disposition.

On this anniversary, therefore, I would honor her by recalling and contemplating the obvious joy with which she lived in time of grievous trial. I would bow once more in reverent memory of her sweet communion with her Lord. And I would be lifted up by her unassuming demonstration of the majesty and the grandeur of a godly faith. I would enfold into ever deeper recesses of my own soul and the best of that to which we both aspired in our purest and holiest moments in union one with the other. And I would recall in grateful memory the triumphant spirit with which she went to her death.

In the commonalities of life with my dear one, soul became knit with dear soul. And there, I was awakened to a new sense of the beauty of divine truth, the exceeding tenderness of divine love, the quiet tranquility of divine peace, and the abiding comfort and joy of divine hope.

In loving memory of Rachel, my Darling,
Edward Humphrey, her devoted husband

Soliloquy on an Unfinished Symphony #5

On our fiftieth (our "Golden Wedding") anniversary
May 23, 1997

In the early fifth century, A.D., the Latin Neoplatonist philosopher, Boethius, falsely accused of treason, lay in prison awaiting execution. While there, he wrote his greatest work, entitled: On the Consolation of Philosophy. In that work, he employed the descriptive and captivating phrase: "this thin and winged moment."

This "thin and winged moment"! How frail and fleeting the sound of those words! And yet, how all-encompassing their grasp of the measure of mortal life in any age—today we are here; tomorrow we are gone. With his incisive words, Boethius has provided an appropriate vehicle for encapsulating my tenderest thoughts on this, the fiftieth anniversary of my union with Rachel, the dearest of earth.

Five years ago today, I shared with her (face-to-face and heart-to-heart) precious, mutual memories from "the swift epic" of our lives together. Unknown to us at the time, this was to be our final anniversary-exchange before the curtain would fall on our temporal bliss. I presented her with a script of my tenderest and holiest thought in her behalf—tense culminating sentiments that had been in process of maturing for nearly half a century. And once again, I stored-up in treasured memory her beautiful response to this overture of love.

Without words (for she had now lost the precious gift of human speech), she disclosed to me something of the silent reaches of her own soul. And together, we ventured reverently into the holy sanctuary of God's love and peace. In her fair countenance, I read once more a love that was constant and pure, a love that knew neither times nor seasons, a love that was stronger than death—a love that will accompany and haunt me down my own solitary journey into the sunset.

In that glorious divine improvisation which had been granted us as the context of our lives in union, we had fallen heir to the many-splendored music of the soul. And here were lingering overtones of lovely themes that had long faded in-and-out to beautify and gladden all our days. Now, we could see that the themes of the beginning (as indeed those of the entire concourse of our journey together) were already merging and vibrating, however imperfectly, in the swelling, pulsating finale.

In that climactic encounter with "the queen of my heart," we experienced what are still to dear memory among the most precious and revealing and enduring moments of our union one with the other. They were, in effect, a veritable denouement of the weaknesses, the fears, the griefs, the joys, and the hopes of our mortality. And all the while, the mystery of dear conjugal love lay shimmering upon the altar!

The story of our lives in union still remains an "Unfinished Symphony." But it, like all things mortal, must await the fullness of Eternal grace to disclose what it might have been, and was not—to God alone be the glory!

In loving memory of Rachel, "my Darling,"
Edward Humphrey, her devoted husband

Soliloquy on an Unfinished Symphony #6

On our fifty-first wedding anniversary
May 23, 1998

Among the many gracious endowments of humankind, none is more precious or sustaining than is that of personal memory. Memory is of course highly selective; and it can be distorted by either willful or unconscious idealization, or by repression. But only memory can restore to us past joys and lost relationships. Only memory can conserve the formative imprint of holy desires and inspired moments of truth and beauty and love. Only priceless memory can stand guard over either the cumulative substance of a single life, or the wisdom of the ages.

On this fifty-first anniversary of my union with the "Darling" of my heart, it is again dear memory that serves me best. Memory restores to me a joyful appearance at the holy altar and the exchange of sacred vows consummating the confluence of two streams to flow henceforth as one. And precious memory keeps alive what was ever the supreme desire of our lives in union—namely, to pursue in holy obedience the revealed divine Will for our lives. In that sweet memory (and, now in reverent solitude), I desire to venture-on in the lure of divine love and godly peace.

Without equivocation, my ultimate creaturely goal is the beholding "in righteousness" the face of my great Creator and Redeemer. With all my soul, I long eventually to be at home with Him—at home in His glorious Presence, at home in His boundless Love, and at home in His holy Will. I wish, meanwhile, to hold all things heavenly in humble and reverent abeyance until my tentative, unrefined faith becomes sight.

And in His glorious Presence, I shall rejoice with "Joy unspeakable and full of glory" if in some manner (as yet incomprehensible to me!) my dear Rachel and I may yet offer together that perfect praise and adoration to which we aspired and never attained in our temporal union. Looking now "as through a glass darkly," my anticipations are no doubt as simplistic as child's play. But Eternal hope has laid hold of my heart and will not let go. With due restraint I dare to believe that in some indefinable sense, sweet memory and holy anticipation are themselves forever wed in the depths of my soul.

Of one thing I rest assured: all things temporal and all things Eternal are secure in the faithful hands of our great and loving God. And with that assurance, I am satisfied. I would not want to become so fixed in my own frail vision of the divine Plan that I do not leave room to be "surprised by joy."

> In loving memory of Rachel, "my Darling"
> Edward Humphrey, her devoted husband

Soliloquy on an Unfinished Symphony #7

On our fifty-second wedding anniversary
May 23, 1999

My heart stands guard over a precious human treasure, a treasure that is not diminished by the toll of the years. It is a dear story of love, a story of blessed conjugal union, a story sublime in all of its fondest reaches. Through precious memory, and despite the intrusion of death itself, this story lives on as an ever-lengthening scroll. In its range and comprehension, it is a story vast beyond the power of mere words to tell.

Like some majestic musical composition, it rings with one lovely melody, though it finds form and expression in varying tempos and in a combination of both major and minor keys, sung or played in harmony. In its special capacity, it offers firm ground for human contentment and peace of mind and heart in my own temporal passage. And to that extent, it surely provides a foregleam of the eternal, for "Love never ends" (I Cor. 13:8).

For me, this day will ever be the most precious of all the year. It commemorates a rendezvous with "my Darling" at the sacred altar. It bears immortal witness to the exchange of life's most inviolable vows. Through a wealth of priceless memory, it holds in trust the reality that all the "moments" of our lives in union (both "the great" ones, and those accounted as but ordinary) were each in their own measure filled with the beauty and the peace and the glory of God. It confirms that though our lives in union were in fact often beset and burdened by stark realities of finite existence, such as are common to humankind, we were never alone, nor were we ever dependent solely upon our own frail resources. He who declared in His incarnate form: "I will not leave you desolate; I will come to you" (John 14:18), expanded that thought in a further wonderful promise. He declared: "If a man loves me, he will keep my word, and my Father will love him, and we will come to him and make our home with him" (John 14:23).

According to His promise, He has been our unfailing comfort and Companion in all the vicissitudes of our journey hitherto. He was my incomparable strength and hope as "my Darling" breathed her latest breath. And He has continued to undergird my solitude with the promise and the joy of "the blessed Hope."

I would now revert once more to a dear passage from the great apostle, Paul—a passage which served throughout our years together as the biblical anchor of our conjugal union. It is Romans, Chapter 8, which we always regarded as a faithful depiction of "life in the Spirit."

In loving memory of Rachel, "my Darling,"
Edward Humphrey, her devoted husband

Appendix C
Letters on the "Anniversary of the Death of Rachel, My Darling"

Ogbomosho, Nigeria
October 24, 1993

The First Anniversary of the Death of Rachel, My Darling

"So Rachel died and she was buried on the way to Ephrath (that is, Bethlehem), and Jacob set up a pillar at her grave; it is the pillar of Rachel's tomb, which is there to this day. Israel [i.e., Jacob] journeyed on..." (Genesis 35:29-21). That was the "graceful and beautiful" Rachel (Genesis 29:17), beloved wife of Jacob, the Hebrew patriarch.

This morning, I awoke to the poignant consciousness that I, too, have "journeyed on" (for the span of a full year) following the death of my own dear Rachel. I, too, left inscribed in stone a marker memorializing the "graceful and beautiful" Rachel who was (and is, and ever shall be!) "my Darling." With that event (except for a deposit of precious and ever-quickening memories), the loveliest chapter of my earthly pilgrimage had drawn to its close. And I was left to find such solace as I might in the anguishing depths of solitude.

That, however, is only the prelude of my meditation on this day of remembering. If that were the whole story, the journey thence (from my own "Ephrath") would have been a lonely and colorless trek. But in the goodness of God, each succeeding day has disclosed its own measure of divine healing and comforting Presence. And in my case, at least, the piercing edges of excruciating pain and grief at the loss of my soul-companion have been somewhat dulled by the unfailing love and support of faithful family members and friends, both old and new. While Christian hope and joy and peace have not removed the pangs of my incomparable loss, they have tempered them and rendered them bearable.

Intermittent shadows still fall athwart my path. But by the grace of God, I "journey on" in the promise and the heartening faith that "the path of the just is as a shining light which shines more and more unto the perfect day" (Proverbs 4:18).

In grateful remembrance,
J. Edward Humphrey, her devoted husband

The Second Anniversary of the Death of Rachel, My Darling

October 24, 1994

Two years ago today, a lovely light in my life flickered, and then went out. For more than forty-five blissful years, its radiance had illumined my path and its soft pure glow had warmed my heart. Now, it was extinguished; its iridescence was eclipsed; its life-nurturing fervency was spent. And though I was never for a moment bereft of a consciousness of divine Presence and comfort, nor of the lure of a blessed hope, I grieved at the absence of my Darling. On this second anniversary of her "home-going," I cherish precious restorative memories of other times when love experienced in fullest measure the inexpressible joy of her dear presence.

On this date a year ago, I awoke early (a great while before dawn), and remembered. I was once more in that very setting which had been the focus of our love and of our earthly vision since the very day we met, now more than half a century ago. After an absence of twenty-eight years (and with no little nostalgia), I had returned to Nigeria, and to the very locale in which the early bonding of faith and divine calling had been experienced and joyfully confirmed. Through the gift of blessed memory, I was now re-living some of the most precious moments of our terrestrial journey together. Indeed, I awoke in the very room in which two of our children were born, and only a room away from that in which our other child was born. I was on the premises of the dearest labor of our lives-the mission station which was "home" to me and my young family for the better part of our seventeen-year span of missionary service. If only my dear Rachel could have been physically present with me there, my joy would have been complete. But, on the other hand, if in the wisdom and the good pleasure of God, the saints in glory are cognizant of mundane matters, I fancy that in the person of my erstwhile soul-companion, there was joy in heaven upon my return to the scene of our former labors.

On this second anniversary of her "home-going," restorative memories still permit me to savor the sweetness and the joy of her lovely presence. At the human level (and for the span of this mortal life), she will continue to be regarded as an incomparable gift of God's love to me. Meanwhile, I have no disposition to presume to possess clear knowledge of the nature or the character of human relations in glory. I am waiting (with appropriate patience, I trust) for the moment of my own translation to become a reality. And then, I reverently desire (if it can be the gracious will of God) to be afforded a heavenly context in which my dear Rachel and I might offer together unhindered love and perfect praise to our great Creator and Redeemer.

In grateful remembrance,
J. Edward Humphrey, her devoted husband

The Third Anniversary of the Death of
Rachel, My Darling

October 24, 1995

Among the dark enigmas of life in this world, there is none that compares with the mystery of human death. Much indeed can be thought and said regarding this perplexing phenomenon without ever really touching the baffling mystery, which enshrouds it. Yet, it lies like a foreboding shadow and pall over the whole of human existence. And no one, however favored, however accomplished, however exalted, however loved, is exempt from its final and cold embrace.

Three years ago on this date, it came as close to me as it can ever come until I am myself its destined prey. In the frailty of helpless finitude, I stood hard-by and beheld in mortal anguish the dearest of earth breathe her latest breath. And in the indescribably precious and comforting company of our two daughters, I uttered a prayer of coronation for "my Darling," even as she made her triumphal entry into the immediate and glorious presence of the Almighty.

When my daughters had quietly (and understandingly) withdrawn from the scene, I bent low for one last tender embrace. And with a depth of love I had never experienced in all our years together, I kissed once more the now pallid cheeks that had long been for me the fairest earthly reflection of the radiant light of God. The life I had known and cherished with all my soul was now swallowed up in death.

With a solemnity reserved for just such a moment, I lingered there for a time at the border between the temporal and the eternal and pondered in the depths of my soul the meaning of both life and death. Each presented to my bewildered soul an impenetrable mystery. In the goodness of God, I had indeed experienced in the company of my dear one something of the beauty and the grace and the glory of life. Life had become in some measure the obsession of my heart in respect of every human creature. But at that moment, I perceived that it will require an eternity to fathom the full depth and range and meaning of life.

254

As for death, its chambers lay cold and silent and unyielding. Whatever secrets it held were not accessible to mortal beings. Not even an echo of the dear life that was, now lingered. Yet, above and beyond the awesome sorrow that had now engulfed me, there was the triumphant assurance that all things temporal (its prizes, its joys, its disappointments, and its losses) still lay "under the aspect of eternity,"—and all was well!

In grateful remembrance,
J. Edward Humphrey, her devoted husband

The Fourth Anniversary of the Death of Rachel, My Darling

October 24, 1996

Mortal death presents itself with many faces. It can come suddenly, as the "grim reaper" or as the "callous destroyer." It can hover barely at arm's length for an unmerciful period of anguishing time, as if to tantalize its prey before pouncing upon it. It can appear as the fearsome companion of deep darkness or as the utter silence of the "no longer." And in any case, its grasp is cold and forbidding. It is indeed "the last enemy." Little wonder that the ancients tended to hypostatize it, attributing to it the character of personal being and standing in dread awe of its lethal majesty.

But even death cannot escape its debt to the service of divine grace. Its sable mantle may well be (and often is!) but a welcome covert of mercy in the darkest hour of human trial. To be human, is to "live one's whole life unto death." Indeed, in the words of the author of the Book of Hebrews, death is by divine appointment (Heb. 9:27). But physical death is never the last word in respect of God's highest creatures.

In the language of Christian faith, those who are in Christ are also "children of the dawn." In faith and the blessed hope, there is that which death itself is powerless to remove or to weaken. In its very shadow, one may confidently exult with the Apostle Paul that death "is swallowed up in victory." And, like Paul, one may continue:

"O death, where is thy victory?
O death, where is thy sting"? (I Cor. 15:14-15)

On this fourth anniversary of the death of my dear soul companion, precious memory and the eternal bond of love preserve inviolate the supreme mortal treasure of my life. For it was at that very juncture that the highest reaches of faith gave way to the sublimest allurement of "the blessed hope." And it was there that I discovered a new urgency in the prayer that our gracious God might hasten to the finish that new creation which He began in Jesus Christ our Lord.

Henceforth, I myself can bear heartfelt witness to the adequacy of the peace and the joy of the divine Presence in our most beleaguered human moment. At that very juncture (I some measure, at least), the temporal is already giving way to the eternal!

"None of us lives to himself, and none of us dies to himself. If we live, we live to the Lord, and if we die, we die to the Lord: so then, whether we live or whether we die, we are the Lord's. For to this end Christ died and lived again that he might be Lord both of the dead and of the living (Rom. 14:7-9).

In grateful remembrance,
J. Edward Humphrey, her devoted husband

The Fifth Anniversary of the Death of
Rachel, My Darling

October 24, 1997

Death reigns in silent majesty over the entire course of nature, including all of mortal being. It is the final frontier-post of all creaturely existence. And in every instance of its inexorable sway, it hangs for itself a veil past which one cannot see. When the apostle Paul was envisioning the final triumph of the risen Christ, he alluded to death as "the last enemy to be destroyed."

But at that very frontier-post of creaturely existence, Christian faith (as faith!), and followed hard by Christian hope, makes its greatest temporal venture. Drawing upon a wealth of divine revelation and treasured dominical promise, it grasps for itself a foregleam of the Eternal:

> "Things beyond our seeing, things beyond our hearing, things beyond our imagining, all prepared by God for those who love him, these it is that God has revealed to us through the Spirit.
>
> For the Spirit explores everything, even the depths of God's own nature...only the Spirit of God knows what God is... This is the Spirit that we have received from God...so that we may know all that God of his own grace gives us" (I Cor. 2:9-13, NEB)

In the context of Christian faith, death may even be regarded as having its own harmonious place in all creaturely existence. It renders all mankind equally poor. It brings to rest every hidden agitation of the redeemed, finite soul. It offers calm to the restless human spirit. It is the medium of transition from the finite to the infinite.

On this fifth anniversary of the death of my dear soul-companion, "eternal life" (not the fear of death!), is the preoccupation of my quieter moments. And divine grace (not the nurturance of grief!), is the dominant motive of my questing soul. In due course, her lovely presence gave way to the beauty and the joy of a world of treasured memory. And that, too, is a precious gift of God. In a slightly altered wording of the thought of Ralph Waldo Emerson, the human heart and its mortal shell are of the dust of the earth; but heart's love is eternal!

Indeed, the story of true conjugal love is an ever-lengthening scroll. And this day is but a reminder that it knows but one melody, even though rendered in varying tempos and employing both major and minor keys in its libretto.

In loving memory of Rachel,
J. Edward Humphrey, her devoted husband

The Sixth Anniversary of the Death of Rachel, My Darling

October 24, 1998

Six years ago today, death wrested from my fond embrace the dearest prize of my mortal being. Utterly helpless to intervene, I could only watch in nameless pain and desperation as that "last enemy" of mankind bore away the dear one with whom I had indeed known primordial oneness. With unrelenting devotion, I accompanied her to the sacred border between the temporal and the eternal. And there, I could only let her go.

Nevertheless, even death could not but bring healing in its sable wings. In the mercy of God, it brought release from the tyranny which had held my dear one captive (in ever increasing intensity) for more than three decades. Death was by no means the final victor, for it was itself being swallowed up in Life! "My Darling" was now set Free! And I fancy that all heaven rejoiced in this her glorious triumph.

The author of the book of Hebrews in the New Testament left to us the sobering admonition: "It is appointed unto man once to die" (Heb. 9:27). To be human is to have at least a vague apprehension of that inevitable, divinely appointed prospect. As fervent adherents of the Christian faith, my dear soul-mate and I had shared our lives in union from the beginning in conscious awareness that we belonged to God, our Creator and Redeemer. We had believed devoutly that His eternal purpose is the one worthy goal of all creaturely existence, including our own. We had sought to know and to conform to His gracious will in the daily ordering of our lives. To serve Him and His holy will was the supreme joy and privilege of our lives. And when our lives in union and our joint-labors were ended, my greatest regret, as the survivor, was (and is!) that we had not been more faithful and productive in our "high calling."

In mortal anguish I stood hardby, my Love
As you, Dear Soul, took your homeward flight.
Whither, then, you winged, my Dove,
Myopic vision followed not.
But I marked well the direction, My Love,
And soon! – so very soon....

In blessed and loving memory of Rachel
(Devoted handmaiden of Christ, her Lord)

J. Edward Humphrey, her devoted husband